W9-AQY-703

CONTENTS

LABORING IN THE HARVEST
LeRoy Eims

NAVPRESS

A MINISTRY OF THE NAVIGATORS
P.O. Box 6000, Colorado Springs, CO 80934

The Navigators is an international Christian organization. Jesus Christ gave His followers the Great
Commission to go and make disciples (Matthew
28:19). The aim of The Navigators is to help fulfill
that commission by multiplying laborers for Christ in
every nation.

NavPress is the publishing ministry of The Navigators.
NavPress publications are tools to help Christians
grow. Although publications alone cannot make disciples or change lives, they can help believers learn
biblical discipleship, and apply what they learn to
their lives and ministries.

AUTHOR

LeRoy Eims is currently serving as Assistant to the President of The Navigators. During his many years with this organization, he has served in a variety of positions, including Director for all the United States ministries.

For many years LeRoy has had a vital interest in winning people to Christ and building them up in the faith. He has traveled throughout the world, ministering on campuses and military bases, and in churches, seminaries, and Bible schools.

LeRoy and his wife, Virginia, live in Colorado Springs.

Other books by LeRoy Eims:
Winning Ways
Be a Motivational Leader
Be the Leader You Were Meant to Be
Wisdom from Above for Living Here Below
No Magic Formula
The Lost Art of Disciple Making
What Every Christian Should Know About Growing
Disciples in Action
Prayer: More Than Words

PREFACE

In May of 1983, Lorne Sanny, the president of The Navigators, and I gave a series of messages on leadership at the Biennial Conference of the Wycliffe Bible Translators.

On our flight home, Lorne commented on the fact that The Navigators had not published any material on the subject of laborers. This seemed strange, since the primary aim of the organization is "to multiply laborers in every nation, thus helping fulfill Christ's Great Commission." And, in our Strategic Global Imperatives we state, "We must always focus on laboring in and laborers for the harvest fields of the world, since this is our calling (Matthew 9:36-38)."

Lorne turned to me and said, "LeRoy, I think you should write a book on the subject." I told him that I felt there were others more qualified than I, but he persisted. This book is the result of that conversation.

As we talked I asked, "If you were to pick one thing you wanted included in the book, what would it be?" His answer was to the point. "Make sure you include the fact that the big trick in working with people is to bring them to the point where they can help others, as opposed to simply needing help themselves." I agreed.

That really is the "big trick." It's the difference between

helping them in their walk with Christ and beginning to help them in their work for Christ. Second Kings 19:30 speaks of taking root downward and bearing fruit upward. That says it succinctly. As we help the new Christians become disciples, we major on getting their roots down into Christ. "Rooted and built up in Him, and established in the faith" (Colossians 2:7). As we help disciples become laborers, we concentrate on helping them become fruitful in evangelism and equipped to help new Christians grow in discipleship.

In this book we will explore the reasons why laborers are the key factor in the work of Christ, why they are central to revival and the Great Commission. We will probe into the problem concerning why they always seem to be in short supply. We will endeavor to discover where they come from and what their mission is.

I send this book forth with the prayer that God will use it to help populate the planet with well-trained, dedicated, spiritually qualified laborers—for the glory of God.

CHAPTER ONE

REVIVE THY WORK

The land was filled with violence. The courts of law were in disrepair. The offended party was condemned and the criminal set free. Business practices were corrupt. There were deep factions separating citizen from citizen. Things seemed to be completely out of control.

The prophet Habakkuk looked out upon the society in which he lived, sickened by what he observed. And so he cried out boldly to his God, "O Lord, revive thy work in the midst of the years, in the midst of the years made known; in wrath remember mercy" (Habakkuk 3:2). It was the cry for revival.

In the summer of 1983 I attended a conference of itinerant evangelists from over 130 countries in Amsterdam. Billy Graham expressed the consensus opinion of the thousands of people attending there: "The greatest need of the hour is the revival of the Church of Jesus Christ." We all joined together at this conference to make the following dedication to the ministry commissioned by Jesus:

> We affirm our commitment to the Great Commission of
> our Lord and declare our willingness to go anywhere, do
> anything, and sacrifice anything God requires of us in the
> fulfillment of that commission.

9

As I look out on the world scene today, I am absolutely convinced that a revival among the people of God would spill over in blessing to the millions without Christ, resulting in hundreds of thousands of lost, alienated, hopeless people being brought to the Savior. Revival of the Church and the Great Commission of Christ are two of the most critical concerns of our day, and these days they seem to be at the forefront of the minds, hearts, and prayers of Christian leaders.

For the past seven years most of my time has been spent outside the framework of the Navigator ministry speaking at Bible schools, seminaries, churches, and conferences sponsored by other Christian organizations. During that time, the two great concerns that have come across loud and clear are (1) the need for revival among the people of God and (2) the need to be engaged in winning the lost and building up the saved in obedience to the Great Commission. I have been hearing these two needs expressed time and again by Church leaders around the world. But how do we follow up our recognition of this urgent need?

One balmy Sunday afternoon in Campinas, Brazil, the Lord gave me a clearer vision of what I can do to help bring about revival among God's people and help fulfill Christ's Great Commission. My wife, Virginia, and I had joined our Brazilian staff for a barbecue at the home of Jim and Marge Petersen, who direct our Navigator work in Latin America. I stepped inside with Aldo Berndt, the leader of Navigator work in Brazil, and we began to discuss the Great Commission.

Aldo asked me if I prayed for revival. I assured him I did. Then he pursued it further. What were the specifics of my prayers?

I told him that I prayed earnestly for a movement of the Holy Spirit that would sweep the world in power, achieving two basic results: the sincere repentance and the moral purification of God's people. I wanted to see the kind of revival that burned off the dross—the wood, hay, and stubble—leaving us "sanctified and meet for the master's use, and prepared unto every good work" (2 Timothy 2:21).

Aldo agreed. But he said that he did one very important thing in addition to that. When I asked what that was, he responded with a question: "When Jesus saw people in need of revival, what did He do?"

"What?" I asked.

Aldo opened his Bible and read Matthew 9:36-38 to me.

When he saw the multitudes, he was moved with compassion on them, because they fainted, and were scattered abroad, as sheep having no shepherd.

Then saith he unto his disciples, The harvest truly is plenteous, but the laborers are few; pray ye therefore the Lord of the harvest, that he will send forth laborers into his harvest.

After Aldo read the passage, he looked right at me and said, "When someone faints, he needs to be revived. Jesus compared the people who came to Him to sheep that had grown weary—collapsed on the ground; panting in the heat of the day; unable to rise; in a pitiful, helpless state. They needed reviving. They needed help from people willing to go into their midst to bring them nourishment, shelter, encouragement, and strength. *Laborers!*"

As I listened to Aldo's words and reflected on his reasoning, I saw the weary sheep and the great Shepherd before my eyes. And I saw a big empty spot that needed to be filled by harvest workers. Jesus clearly demonstrated that revival cannot be separated from the need for laborers.

Ever since that conversation with Aldo, I have given a great deal of thought to what he said. I have researched the Scriptures for more light on the idea of revival through laboring. I know that we are called to pray for results in the harvest field. Yet if I am disposed to pray for revival but am saturated with pride and arrogance, I might as well save my breath to cool my soup. The high, holy, and eternal God hears and answers only those who are humble about their accomplishments and contrite about their sins.

> For thus saith the high and lofty One that inhabiteth eternity, whose name is Holy; I dwell in the high and holy place, with him also that is of a contrite and humble spirit, to revive the spirit of the humble, and to revive the heart of the contrite ones. (Isaiah 57:15)

We need revival to refresh our sometimes stale spirits. The psalmist wisely prayed, "Wilt thou not revive us again: that thy people may rejoice in thee?" (Psalm 85:6). The psalmist freely admitted his faint and feeble condition, and also acknowledged that God's reviving power was his hope. He looked forward to the day when he would experience the special visitation of the Holy Spirit on his soul, at which time a holy joy would flood his life. I'm sure the psalmist was not disappointed, for joy follows revival as sure as morning follows night.

In the 138th Psalm, David recorded an interesting insight. "Though I walk in the midst of trouble, thou wilt revive me: thou shalt stretch forth thine hand against the wrath of mine enemies, and thy right hand shall save me" (Psalm 138:7). God often gets our undivided attention during the times of our sorrows, using them as the catalyst to energize us in the life of holiness and blessing. And if, through pain, suffering, and sorrow, we are revived, then we can truly rejoice in the Lord.

As you reflect on these passages, you might wonder just where Aldo and his emphasis on laborers fit into this whole scheme. Let's turn the coin over and study the other side for a bit. Remember: it was not Aldo who came up with the connection between fainting sheep and laborers. Jesus did that. But just what *is* the connection and how does it fit?

In executing His work, God has two means available: natural and supernatural, ordinary and extraordinary. I have seen this double thrust of God at work many times. Take, for instance, the matter of healing. A number of my friends have come down with various illnesses and have gone to the hospital or have been placed under a doctor's care. In response to the prayers of His people, God has healed many of them through a natural healing course. On the other hand, I have seen cases of direct intervention in the form of immediate supernatural healing.

When I was three years old in the Lord, I observed a most remarkable act of divine healing. A minister had suffered for months with a wound that would not heal. He was due to go back to the hospital on a Friday night for surgery on Saturday morning. The following Sunday I happened to be attending this pastor's church. The bulletin announced the visiting preacher— but about a half hour before the morning service was to begin, the pastor, who was scheduled to be in the hospital, showed up at the church, walking up and down the aisles of the sanctuary shaking hands with people and joyfully telling them his story.

On the previous Thursday night, the pastor and the elders of the church had met for prayer. The elders had anointed him with oil and prayed for him—as the pastor put it, "in the scriptural fashion." Friday he went to the hospital fully expecting to be operated on Saturday morning. The wound was draining so badly that when they changed the bandage for the last time late Friday night, the drainage was so profuse that the sheets on the bed were stained and had to be replaced.

Saturday morning came and the pastor awakened early. He felt the outside of the bandage, and to his surprise it was perfectly dry. He then did something medically unacceptable. He put his contaminated hand down underneath the bandage, and discovered that there was no wound. It was completely healed.

He immediately leaped out of bed, tore off the bandage, and, sure enough, the wound was healed, and, furthermore, there was not even a scar! He went to the telephone to call one of the doctors (who was a member of the church where he was pastor), but decided against it since calling at 5:00 A.M. seemed a bit early. So he left word with the nurse to ask the doctor to come in to see him before he prepared for surgery.

Around 8 A.M. the doctor came in and asked, "What's the problem?" The pastor said, pointing to the place where the wound used to be, "That's the problem: There is no problem! I'm totally healed!" The doctor took a long, careful look at the formerly infected spot, poked around, and asked if it hurt. "Why should it hurt?" the pastor replied. "There's nothing there!"

The doctor then placed a call to his fellow surgeon—who by this time was waiting in surgery—and asked him to come to the pastor's room. He walked in and asked, "What's the trouble?" "That's the trouble," the doctor replied. "There is no trouble!" And sure enough! The second doctor looked it all over . . . poked around . . . asked if it hurt. And when he discovered that the pastor was completely healed, he said, with tears in his eyes, "Pastor, you've been talking to the right Person."

God had simply performed a supernatural act of physical healing, for which He received all the glory. And through this miracle, many people came to Christ as the story spread through the hospital to nurses, doctors, and staff. Many Christians who worked at the hospital had a great time witnessing for the next few months.

God uses two primary means to accomplish His purposes on this earth—the ordinary and the extraordinary. Is it possible that God's ordinary means of infusing the new life of revival includes you and me as His instruments in this task? Along with Habakkuk, you and I look out on the world in all its corruption and wickedness, and we conclude that there is no other solution but *God.* With Isaiah we have seen that God uses His Word to comfort and convict the humble and contrite. And with the psalmist we have seen how God brings us people in need who have been brought low through the sorrows, bumps, and blasts of daily life.

As various facets of spiritual reality are brought to light, the need for laborers and the reason for Jesus' command to pray for them becomes more and more obvious. We should not only pray for God to do something spectacular and extraordinary, but we should also synchronize in with His *ordinary* means of accomplishing His work.

But all too often we pray and plead with God for revival, while we impatiently wait for Him to act *supernaturally.* At the same time, God in heaven is usually waiting patiently for *us* to act. He wants to use us as His ordinary means to revive His people and to evangelize the rest of the world.

When Jesus looked on the multitude, His heart was moved with love and compassion. Two pictures came into His mind. The first was a picture of a flock of sheep—hopeless, helpless, and exhausted. Revival was certainly the need of the hour. "When someone faints, he needs to be revived."

The second picture that came into His mind was that of an abundant harvest—a huge, overripe field of grain that needed to be gathered in.

And what is Jesus' diagnosis as He looks out on our world today? Does He still observe helpless sheep and a field of overripe grain that needs to be gathered in? As we look about our world today—Europe, Africa, Asia, the Americas—we see that literally billions of people are without Christ. A vast harvest field indeed! Jesus still challenges us to pray for laborers to harvest that global field.

Two things happen when we accept Jesus' challenge to pray for laborers. First, God responds to our prayers by raising up those laborers. He desires far more than we do to bring in the harvest. But there is also a second interesting result that is kind of a byproduct. As we pray for laborers, our own hearts become stirred *to be those laborers.*

Billy Graham described laborers as those who have been "filled, anointed, and called by the Holy Spirit, and who are in turn witnessing for Him wherever God sends them." But a laborer is also moved with compassion over the diverse needs of the people of God—people who have been brought low by the blows of life and need help in regaining their joyful walk with the Lord.

To accomplish this double thrust, what must we do? We must labor to win the lost and do all we can through prayer and every other means possible to see spiritually qualified laborers multiplied to the glory of God. The stakes are high. Revival is not optional. Millions of fainting, distressed, helpless people need a fresh, energizing touch of God in their lives as the Holy Spirit ministers the Word of God to them through those for whom Christ told us to pray: *laborers.* The Great Commission— with its twofold emphasis of evangelizing the lost and edifying the saved—must capture our thoughts, our prayers, our time.

"O Lord, revive thy work in the midst of the years, in the midst of the years made known." May God revive His work *and* His workers!

CHAPTER TWO

A SHORTAGE OF FIELD HANDS

Laborers are few. They were few in Jesus' day and they're few today. Churchgoers are many. Seminars are many. Conferences are many. Religious institutes are many. Programs are many. But laborers are few.

Why does this situation persist year after year, decade after decade, century after century? Why are there never enough laborers? There seem to be five basic reasons.

First, if the devil decided to attack the foremost strategic element in revival and world evangelization, where do you think he would strike? Where would he concentrate his efforts? Would he mobilize his forces in order to concentrate on some peripheral issue? No, he would strike at the heart of the matter. Like a mad dog he would go for the jugular vein, hitting where it would hurt the most.

Try to imagine the impact of a church on a neighborhood if every member of that church was a spiritually qualified, dedicated laborer, totally given over to Christ and His cause. What would it be like if the work of Christ was being handled not just by a few professionals—the divinely appointed leadership of the Church—but by thousands, hundreds of thousands, millions of highly trained, motivated, mature, fruitful, well-

17

equipped laymen and laywomen? Our churches need people whose greatest desire is to discover and fulfill God's will for their lives—laborers who upon leaving the sanctuary each Sunday go out into the world with the consuming desire to know Christ and to make Him known.

We know that the results of such a laboring force would be staggering. The devil knows that, too. And I believe that's where he concentrates his efforts. He will get us bickering among ourselves over silly, pointless, worthless issues while millions go to a Christless grave. He will get us spending our time on many good activities while we leave the very best undone, involved in work that is only remotely related to the Great Commission of Christ—to make known the gospel and to make disciples.

What is our best source of power to counterattack? Of course, it is the power of Christ Himself. Jesus clearly demonstrated His power over the devil and all his forces (Mark 5:1-13). And what did Jesus tell *us* to do? His solution was astoundingly simple. He told us to pray, for we cannot overcome the powers of evil by strictly human means. No amount of human effort will turn the tide. Why? Because the battle is spiritual, and a spiritual battle must be fought with spiritual weapons.

Paul said, "For though we walk in the flesh, we do not war after the flesh: (For the weapons of our warfare are not carnal, but mighty through God to the pulling down of strong holds)" (2 Corinthians 10:3-4). Christian, make no mistake about it: This *is* warfare—warfare for the very highest stakes, fought on a global scale. You and I must be armed to the teeth.

Listen again to Paul: "Finally, my brethren, be strong in the Lord, and in the power of his might. Put on the whole armour of God, that ye may be able to stand against the wiles of the devil. For we wrestle not against flesh and blood, but against principalities, against powers, against the rulers of the darkness of this world, against spiritual wickedness in high places" (Ephesians 6:10-12). So be done with lesser things. Have no trust in the wisdom of this world.

The Bible tells us that "the world by wisdom knew not God" (1 Corinthians 1:21). Now I ask you, Since the world does not even *know* God, would it not be madness to turn to the world to discover how to do His work? Go to the Source. Trust the Lord Himself. Pray that through the power of Christ the devil will be bound (Mark 3:27). Pray that Satan's efforts to retard the growth of laborers will be overcome.

The second reason why laborers are few is found in the nature of the term itself. There is something unpleasant in the idea of being a laborer. By nature we would rather be a supervisor, manager, director, or executive—*anything* but a common laborer! And that is exactly the meaning of the word that Jesus used. "A field hand." "An agricultural worker." "One who works for hire." How unpleasant! How degrading to see ourselves as nothing but field hands in the harvest! Humanly speaking, a common laborer is the *last* thing we would want to be.

This truth was brought forcibly to my attention a few years ago in northern Germany. I had set aside a few days from my ministry trip to try to discover my roots. I knew that my father had come to the United States from Germany but I was uncertain as to the exact location. Oldenberg was on his birth certificate, but when I went there I was told that years ago Oldenberg also referred to that whole part of the country, sort of a state or province.

But the man in charge of records said that there was one more thing that might help us: He could check Napoleon's tax records to see if there was anyone named Eims listed. And sure enough! There were three people by that name and they were all from the extreme north—up near the coast of the North Sea. So he began to bring huge record books from that section and we began to go through those tomes page by page.

Two days of turning pages proved fruitless, but on the afternoon of the third day I found it. There was my grandfather's name: Hero Fakin Eims! I was so excited that I called out to Virginia and to John Advocaat, a Navigator staff man in Germany who was helping us, "I found it!" They came hurrying over to see my discovery—and so did the man in charge. By this time he too had become quite interested in the search. There, in handwritten nineteenth century German, were some basic details of my grandfather's life—where and when he was born, his occupation, and so on.

As he read, suddenly his face fell from excitement to pity. "Oh, I'm so sorry," he said. He had come to the column that told my grandfather's occupation. "Oh," he said, "this is terrible." "Good grief," I thought. "I wonder if Granddad was a horse thief." What could be so terrible to cause the man such chagrin? "What was he?" I asked. "Oh," he said, "I'm so ashamed to tell you—your grandfather was . . . a common laborer!" My grandfather apparently drove a team of mules pulling a freight wagon. He helped build the dikes of northern Germany. In the language of the American frontier, my grandfather was a mule skinner.

Unlike the German record keeper, I was absolutely elated! I exulted in the fact that my granddad spent his days in honest, hard work. But I could understand the man's chagrin. I'm sure he felt sorry for me. Here was this American who had spent all this time looking for his ancestors only to discover that they were nothing but common laborers. That's the way the world thinks.

But as I consider my own background, I am truly thankful for the days I spent in the hot, dusty fields of an Iowa farm—cultivating corn, putting up hay, and so on. Admittedly it was hot, hard, dirty work, but there is something noble in that—and vitally important. The world does not get fed unless the field hand does his work. Somebody *must* harvest the crop. When the grain is ripe it must be brought in. There is nothing humiliating about being the one who performs that labor.

This is the picture that Jesus paints for us. In Matthew 9:36-38, He is not talking about sowing, cultivating, weeding, and preparing the soil by plowing and harrowing; He is talking about reaping a stand of grain that is ready to be gathered in. You and I must ask ourselves, Am I ready to dedicate myself to that task? Or do I shy away from being an ordinary field hand in the kingdom of God? Do I feel that such a ministry is below my station in life? If so, remember this: Jesus was a laborer. He said, "I must work the works of him that sent me, while it is day: the night cometh, when no man can work" (John 9:4).

The apostles too were laborers. Do you recall what Jesus said in John 4:34-38?

> Jesus saith unto them, My meat is to do the will of him that sent me, and to finish his work. Say not ye, There are yet four months, and then cometh harvest? Behold, I say unto you, Lift up your eyes, and look on the fields; for they are white already to harvest. And he that reapeth receiveth wages, and gathereth fruit unto life eternal: that both he that soweth and he that reapeth may rejoice together.

Do I shy away because I know a laborer has it tough? A laborer gets blisters. His feet get sore, his back aches, the sun scorches his skin, and the dust of the field gets in his nose and mouth. But even though all this is true, the words of Jesus still stand. The need has not changed—unless possibly to become greater. For the work of the harvest laborer is the strategic key for meeting the truly great needs of this world—for the revival of the Church and for the execution of the Great Commission of Jesus Christ.

A third reason for the lack of laborers is shortsightedness. Although we see the cost, we fail to see the rewards. We must remember that the cost is high for anything that is truly valuable. A new Mercedes costs more than a ten-year-old Ford Pinto. But when you own one, you have something that will last. So it is with a laborer. Laborers are invaluable, indispensable, and irreplaceable in God's great plan.

Three years ago I met a woman who was about ready to give up. Her life had virtually fallen apart. Enter a laborer, who began to pray for the woman. Soon she began to go to lunch with her and share the Scriptures. Then they set up a regular weekly luncheon date to pray together. Soon they were doing Bible study together and the woman began to memorize Scripture.

A fresh breeze began to revive her crushed and sorrowing soul. Joy replaced sadness; hope replaced despair; peace replaced inner turmoil. She began to get her spiritual roots down into Christ. She began to grow.

Other Christian women who had known her began to ask questions. What has happened to Gwen? What has happened in her life to bring this remarkable change? Simple. A laborer came into her life, who, under the guidance and blessing of the Holy Spirit, was used of God to bring the ministry of Christ to her troubled soul. She was revived.

Jesus was trying to describe this ministry of the laborer to those who had gathered in the synagogue in Nazareth one Sabbath day. He read from Isaiah:

> The Spirit of the Lord God is upon me; because the Lord
> hath anointed me to preach good tidings unto the meek;
> he hath sent me to bind up the brokenhearted, to pro-
> claim liberty to the captives, and the opening of the pris-
> on to them that are bound; to proclaim the acceptable
> year of the Lord, and the day of vengeance of our God; to

comfort all that mourn; to appoint unto them that mourn
in Zion, to give unto them beauty for ashes, the oil of joy
for mourning, the garment of praise for the spirit of heav-
iness; that they might be called trees of righteousness, the
planting of the Lord, that he might be glorified. (Isaiah
61:1-3)

And now, bless God, Gwen has become a "tree of righteousness." Her life has begun to bear fruit and she is passing on
to others the ministry that the Holy Spirit brought to her
through a faithful laborer. One more laborer has been added to
the kingdom of God. Was it a costly process? Of course! Hours
on the phone—often at very inconvenient times. Hours in
prayer—for her and with her. Hours spent in Bible study—in
exhortation, edification, and comfort. But nobody said it would
be easy. When a laborer goes out into the field, it is no surprise
to him that the weather is hot and muggy, that the work is hard
and the hours long. That's his life.

I have a very special friend who is serving the Lord as a
foreign missionary. One day someone asked him how he copes
with the fact that he is always fighting a fever or some sort of
stomach problem. "Yes," he said, "I know that my stomach is
being eaten out. I know that my life will probably be shortened
by five or ten years. But is that too high a price to pay to see
laborers raised up who can be used of God to bring salvation
and hope to millions of the poor, sick, sorrowing people of the
world? I don't think so."

My missionary friend, incidentally, could quite easily be
doing something else. He has a Ph.D. in Solid-state Physics from
a prestigious university. He could be living a life of ease in
some prominent position in the academic world. But he has
become a laborer in the harvest, for God has sent him to
destitute village people. He has a vision of seeing hundreds of
thousands of laborers raised up whose lives and ministry will

change the face of the land. It is his plan to see a laborer within walking distance of anyone who is spiritually hungry for Christ and His Word. His means of doing this? Prayer and hard work. His strategy? Spiritual multiplication, which we will look at later.

A fourth reason for the laborer shortage is prayerlessness. We usually don't obey the command of Jesus. We fail to fervently pray to the Lord of the harvest to send out laborers. This was the frank admission of a carload of pastors who were attending a five-day disciplemaking seminar at a seminary in their city. I asked the class members to discuss among themselves the problem of the shortage of laborers and to give their reasons for the shortage in our first session the following day.

When I asked the question the next day, one of the men stood; he had been elected spokesman for the group. All five of the men had agreed on the reason. His answer was to the point: "We have agreed that laborers are few because of our own prayerlessness." He sat down. The men turned, looked at each other, and nodded in agreement. The looks on their faces told me they felt an honest sense of shame and remorse. They were not proud of their answer.

If you doubt that prayerlessness is a major reason for the shortage of laborers, let me ask *you* a question. What place does the prayer for laborers occupy in your life? Do you pray for laborers? Do you know *anybody* who makes this a priority in prayer?

Isn't it interesting that this is usually the case with things that are truly basic? Rather than read the Bible, we read books about the Bible. Rather than pray, we worry. Rather than witness, we soothe our conscience by paying the pastor to do it for us. And rather than pray for laborers, we occupy ourselves with busywork. We love to complicate things. Jesus' solution seems too simple.

The fifth and final reason for the laborer shortage is not quite so easy to explain, but here goes. Laborers are few because the majority of the Christian world does not even realize there is such a class of people in the Bible. They know there are new converts. They know of disciples. They know there are Christian workers—missionaries, preachers, Christian leaders. But laborers are an unknown entity. They are usually completely overlooked.

Recently I received a publication that contained an interview led by a good friend of mine with five leading pastors from various parts of the world. The topic: Revival and world evangelization. The primary question of the interview: What does your church need in order to bring about revival and a greater impact for Christ in world evangelization in your part of the world? The answer? Two things: We need more disciples and more leaders. I would agree.

But one element was noticeably absent in this interview. There was no mention of a core of spiritually qualified laborers. Why? Because these men were not thinking in that direction.

Jesus had numerous disciples. Many people followed Him as eager learners. He had His apostles, who made up His leadership team. But He also had "the Seventy." Who were they? Apparently they were unsung, unheralded, and unknown, but competent to labor with practically the same job description Jesus had given "the Twelve." (Compare Matthew 10 with Luke 10.) No official position. No prestigious titles. Just a lot of hard work to do. Field hands. And there were only seventy of them. They were few, but they were effective.

Isn't that what we need today? Visualize your church with a band of laborers who are competent to minister to the needs of people, equipped to reach the lost and edify the saved. Laborers whose lives are given over completely to God and whose focus is the Great Commission to make disciples of all nations. May their tribe greatly increase!

CHAPTER THREE

A JOB DESCRIPTION FOR LABORERS

For many years the Muruts of the jungles of Sarawak, East Malaysia, were savage headhunters. With the introduction of Western culture, the tribe was almost wiped out by alcohol. Then, bless God, some laborers from Australia showed up. Now nearly half of the thirty thousand Murut people profess faith in Christ.

An American with a Ph.D. in Anthropology was sent by a prestigious university to study the Muruts. Instead of a tribe suffering from the ravages of alcohol and the bloody wars of the headhunters, he found a group of people in good health, living a lifestyle he greatly admired. He lived with the tribe for a year in their longhouses, and, after observing the effects of the gospel, he gave his life to Christ there in the Sarawak jungle. The power of the gospel to change the heart is undeniable. As Scripture says, "If any man be in Christ, he is a new creature: old things are passed away; behold, all things are become new" (2 Corinthians 5:17). The gospel does so much good that it's a crying shame more people aren't out there spreading it around.

George Mueller was a man of faith used by God to provide clothing, food, and shelter for thousands of neglected orphans in the 1800s. Was he always such a benevolent soul, dedicating himself totally to the care of the poor and needy? No. As a young man he lived only for himself. He was a thief. He wrote, "I do not remember that at any time when my sins were found out, it made any other impression on me than to make me think how I might do the thing the next time more cleverly, so as not to be detected."

On the day of his mother's death, George got drunk in a tavern and "went about the streets, half intoxicated." On the day he was confirmed in the church, he was "guilty of gross immorality." At times he tried to reform. "But," he writes, "as I attempted the thing in my own strength, all soon came to nothing, and I still grew worse." He was thrown in jail for fraud and theft. After some time he was released and continued his "dissipated life." He was greatly in debt. He cheated people out of their money and borrowed from friends with no intention of repaying them.

The story goes on and on, but the point is this: At times Mueller felt he should try to reform. He even made a few feeble attempts, but nothing worked. Then he heard the gospel and he was converted. He wrote, "Now my life became very different, though all sins were not given up at once. My wicked companions were given up, the going to taverns was entirely discontinued. The habitual practice of telling falsehoods was no longer indulged in." He no longer lived in habitual sin. "I read the Scriptures, prayed often, loved the brethren, went to church from right motives and stood on the side of Christ, though laughed at by my fellow students."

That was the beginning of a life devoted solely to helping helpless orphans. What was it that transformed the immoral thief and liar into one of the great men in the history of the Church? What caused such a radical change in his life? The gospel! We should never be surprised at such dramatic changes in a person's life. For the Bible tells us of many such transformations.

> Know ye not that the unrighteous shall not inherit the
> kingdom of God? Be not deceived: neither fornicators,
> nor idolaters, nor adulterers, nor effeminate, nor abusers
> of themselves with mankind, nor thieves, nor covetous,
> nor drunkards, nor revilers, nor extortioners, shall inherit
> the kingdom of God. And such were some of you: but ye
> are washed, but ye are sanctified, but ye are justified in
> the name of the Lord Jesus, and by the Spirit of our God.
> (1 Corinthians 6:9-11)

It was the *gospel* that made the difference. You know, the gospel
does so much good that it's a crying shame more people aren't
out there spreading it around.

During the Amsterdam '83 conference, the daily newspapers
reported the fierce fighting and escalation of the war in
Lebanon. Many died. The Jews blamed the Syrians. The Lebanese blamed the Syrians. The Syrians blamed the Jews and the
Lebanese. There was no trust. The land was filled with deep
bitterness resulting from decades of hatred, suspicion, and
brutality.

During this Middle East turmoil, something took place at
the conference that clearly spoke of the real solution to the
problem. At a small table three men sat together sipping coffee,
enjoying each other's fellowship, men whose lives had been
transformed by the power of the gospel. Three men: a Jew, a
Lebanese, and a Syrian. What millions of dollars invested in
manmade solutions could not do, what hundreds of hours
spent in secular negotiations could not do, what thousands of
miles of travel by the keenest diplomats on both sides could
not do, the Godmade solution of the *gospel* had done. Through
the power of the gospel, wounds were healed, hate was overcome by love, and people from three warring nations sat
together as friends. In the context of Jesus Christ and His

gospel, these men were no longer "strangers and foreigners, but fellow-citizens with the saints, and of the household of God" (Ephesians 2:19). The gospel does so much good it is a crying shame more people aren't out spreading it around.

Do you know why the gospel is not spread around more than it is? Because there is a shortage of laborers, those persevering gospel-spreaders of the kingdom of God. Many people don't have a clear idea of what a laborer is and does. Here are some basic principles, a few do's and don'ts out of my own experience, that might serve as a broad job description for harvest laborers.

A LABORER PERSEVERES. If at first you don't succeed, try, try again. Did you invite your neighbors to a backyard barbecue without receiving a response? Okay, try inviting them to a football game, or to the beach, or to the ski slopes. Did you try to interest your next-door neighbors in a Bible study to no avail? Okay, try the couple across the street.

Recently I was on my way to Dallas to speak to a gathering of Wycliffe Bible Translators. I boarded the plane in Colorado Springs, and my seatmates were a tall, muscular young man and his wife. He was a policeman on his way to Honolulu to testify at a trial. When I began to witness to them, I discovered they were both Christians.

Our plane landed in Denver to take aboard passengers for our nonstop flight to Dallas. That meant I had approximately thirty minutes on the ground before we took off. I began roaming up and down the aisle looking for someone to witness to. I began a conversation with a young Air Force lieutenant but soon discovered he was a Christian also. By this time the Denver passengers began to get on the plane. My new seatmate was a young engineer from North Dakota. He was not a Christian, so I had a marvelous time sharing the gospel with him. The lesson to be learned: Persevere.

A LABORER IS PREPARED. Not long ago I heard a Masai tribesman from Africa give his testimony. He told how he had been converted, and then he gave a demonstration of how to hunt lions with a spear. The critical time is when the lion leaps, at which time the spear is released. When asked, "What happens if you miss?" the Masai hunter thought for a moment and then said, "If I miss the lion, my family misses me."

When I heard this man state a principle of life and death so matter of factly, I related it to witnessing. That's true, isn't it? Often we get just one good opportunity. If we are to follow Paul's admonition to share God's word "in season and out of season" (2 Timothy 4:2), we must follow Peter's command to "be ready always" (1 Peter 3:15).

Recently a man was shot in the chest during a gun battle between two forces in a city in Central America. He was found lying on the sidewalk by a taxi driver who picked him up, put him in his cab, and drove him to the hospital. On the way to the hospital, the man who was shot shared the gospel with the taxi driver and led him to Christ. He was a prepared laborer.

A LABORER BUILDS BRIDGES. Many people in the world today have no interest at all in what Jesus did and taught. The spiritual climate in the Reformation countries of Europe has been described as more than just cold toward the gospel. Kenneth Kantzer called it a "spiritual ice age." Jim Petersen, upon visiting Germany, observed that the influence of the Church is exhausted. Those of us who travel in that part of the world are saddened to see that the great cathedrals, once filled with spiritually hungry people, are now practically empty.

How can we appeal to the people who have become disillusioned with "church"? A dedicated laborer will try to build bridges to them. But from what materials will he build these bridges? Let me suggest a few spiritual building materials that various laborers have found to be quite effective.

1. *Love others.* Christian love manifests itself in respect for people as individuals, with kindness and tolerance for their ignorance of spiritual truth and patience toward their pagan lifestyle.

2. *Live a positive Christian life.* Demonstrate that Christ is in you by living the pure lifestyle of a citizen of the kingdom of God.

3. *Be knowledgeable.* Try your best to have a grasp of Christian answers to the meaning and purpose of life, personal difficulties, and the desire for freedom and joy.

4. *Rely on the Holy Spirit.* Constantly trust in the guidance, wisdom, and power of the Holy Spirit. He will help you gain a confidence in and a dedication toward the Scriptures and prayer.

5. *Listen to others.* Take seriously what they think, say, and believe, respecting their sincerity.

6. *Show concern.* A few months ago in Indonesia one of our laborers, while driving his car, hit a Muslim lady on a bicycle. He took her to the hospital, took care of her for weeks, paid all her bills, and provided for all her needs. The lady's husband was dumbfounded by the care and concern shown to his wife. Through it all the laborer was able to share the gospel with them. They saw his honest concern and related it to the teachings of Christ. Today the couple is in a Bible study and very close to the kingdom of God.

7. *Don't condemn.* The lifestyle of others may be offensive, but we are witnesses, not judges. To the woman taken in adultery Jesus said, "Neither do I condemn thee." Try to understand the way of life and value system of other people.

8. *Rejoice in the Lord.* The outcome of witnessing is not always positive and successful. Rejection and suffering are part of the laborer's experience as well. Even so, we have reason in Christ to rejoice always.

9. *Be firm and yet flexible.* Kenneth Latourette in his

History of the Expansion of Christianity says that one of the reasons for the amazing success and expansion of the early Church was its ability to be both intransigent and pliable at the same time. It refused to compromise with the social customs and moral practices of the day. "This," Latourette says, "gave the Christians a source of strength in their convictions and a zeal in winning converts. It was adaptable, but on essentials refused to compromise."

The early Christians refused to participate in many of the culturally accepted practices, both religious and social, that the unbelievers accepted as a normal and desirable part of life. The apostle Peter wrote concerning the pagans of that period, "They think it strange that ye run not with them to the same excess of riot, speaking evil of you" (1 Peter 4:4). These people thought it very irregular that the Christians no longer practiced what was common in their society.

Paul told the Christians in Thessalonica, "We beseech you, brethren, that ye increase more and more; and that ye study to be quiet, and to do your own business, and to work with your own hands, as we commanded you" (1 Thessalonians 4:10-11). Later he told these same people, "For even when we were with you, this we commanded you, that if any would not work, neither should he eat" (2 Thessalonians 3:10). Such thoughts were social dynamite to the Greeks of that day, who regarded all manual labor as the occupation of a slave. No self-respecting Greek worked with his hands. It was unheard of.

Equally surprising to the Greeks were Paul's words to them in 1 Thessalonians 4:7: "For God hath not called us unto uncleanness, but unto holiness." Chastity was an absolutely foreign virtue, almost completely unknown in Greek society. The Christians were unmovable on Christian virtues, but flexible in their efforts to reach out to the pagans around them.

10. *Don't make a nuisance of yourself.* Recently on an airplane I began to witness to my seatmate. Immediately he put

on his stereo headset and turned his face to the window. I shut up. I could see he was in no mood to talk about spiritual matters. I prayed for him, committed him to the Lord, and settled back to read a book.

One of the primary rules of witnessing is to try to leave the door open for the next witness. Don't turn the person off by making a nuisance of yourself. We are fishers of men. A fisherman dangles some bait in front of the fish and then hopes the fish is interested. When Moses saw the burning bush he became interested. "And Moses said, I will now turn aside, and see this great sight, why the bush is not burnt" (Exodus 3:3). God did not lasso him. But He got his attention and Moses responded.

11. *Don't be controlled by unwarranted fears.* The Bible says, "God hath not given us the spirit of fear; but of power, and of love, and of a sound mind" (2 Timothy 1:7). Of course we are afraid from time to time. But we must not live under a "spirit of fear." We should be controlled by God.

Recently Virginia and I were on a ministry tour through Mexico, Central America, and South America. One night we were awakened by what sounded like a pitched battle in the street near our hotel. I sat there in bed reflecting on the anti-American hostility I had seen in the magazines and newspapers the day before. I could hear ack-ack guns, mortar fire, hand grenades, automatic rifles, and machine guns. That night we slept very little, wondering who was fighting and if we were safe.

The next day there was no sign of a battle, so we went to a nearby restaurant for lunch. Halfway through the meal the noise began again. I asked the waiter what was going on. He said it was fireworks being set off to celebrate the birth of one of their most important saints. It was a happy fiesta.

For many hours I had been controlled by unfounded fears that robbed me of my peace of mind and my sleep. What I had envisioned as a military conflict was actually a birthday party. In like manner, too many Christians are robbed of many fine opportunities to witness because of their unwarranted and unfounded fears about an encounter they have never experienced.

12. *Don't speak in riddles.* Religious language is often unintelligible to the unsaved. We must use words they understand.

One night last year I was staying in a motel in Rockwell, Illinois. The TV program guide described what was being shown on HBO. It said the show was filled with "adult situations" and "adult language." I didn't turn the TV on but I knew what it meant. "Adult situations" means the show is shot through with immorality. "Adult language" really means foul, dirty, crude, and blasphemous speech. But that's not what it said. I had to decipher it. Such double-talk should never be true of our Christian witness. The person to whom we are witnessing should be able to understand exactly what we are saying. Terms such as "born again," "saved," "repentance," and "receive Christ" are biblically sound but often unintelligible to the nonChristian. Make your message as plain, direct, and clear as possible.

I watched this principle of communication in action one night in Boulder, Colorado. A man had just robbed a local convenience food store and the police had caught him. The three plainclothes policemen were very clear in their communication with the robber. "Hold it right there! Come out of the car with your hands up! Get out! Get out! Slowly! Get down on your knees! Now! Now! Keep your hands up! Don't move!" One of the policemen monitored the whole procedure from the corner of the building with a gun pointed directly at the robber.

At first we thought it was a couple of college guys just goofing around, but we soon learned better. We quickened our pace and got out of there. The robber knew it was no joke. And he knew exactly what he was supposed to do. No one had to decipher it for him. The cops spoke very plainly. It is important that we too are prepared with clear, concise language.

Recently a young man showed up at the office of a veterinarian friend of mine, Dr. Bob Taussig. The young man said, "I have heard that you can explain religious matters. I have a pet snake, an eight-foot python. It sleeps on my bed. But recently something has begun to happen that frightens me. Daily I feel compelled to bow down to it. I kneel by the bed and stare into its eyes. I have begun to worship the snake and I am frightened. I've been to a Jewish rabbi, a Catholic priest, and a Protestant minister, and none of them can tell me what to do. Can you help me?"

"Yes," Bob said, "first of all, get rid of the snake." Then Bob gave him the gospel. In a few days the young man returned. He had gotten rid of the snake, had accepted Christ, and brought Bob a thank-you gift. What the young man needed was clear instructions in words he could understand. Prominent on the job description of a laborer is the spreading of the gospel message—in straightforward language.

The global need for the gospel shows up in many ways in many places as greed, hate, lust, and deceit abound. We hear the stories every day in the news media of man's inhumanity to man. A recent example of the compelling worldwide need for the gospel is an incident that took place on the streets of Calcutta. A taxi was roaring through the streets when suddenly a cow stepped out into the street from the sidewalk on the left side (the side on which they drive in India). At the same time a young girl stepped out into the street from the sidewalk on the right. The driver had a split-second decision to make. Which would he kill? Of course, if you know anything about the religions of India, you know which way he swerved. He couldn't kill the cow; it was a god. Fortunately a man reached out and flung the little girl out of the way of the taxi, thus saving her life.

Millions today live in the darkness of false religion, superstition, and fear. The harvest is plenteous. The laborers are few. Pray the Lord of the harvest to thrust forth laborers into this vast, overripe harvest.

CHAPTER FOUR

THE PRINCIPLES OF COMMITMENT

Last year Virginia and I were in Australia on a ministry trip. Our last stop was a Navigator staff meeting at a conference center an hour or so from Sydney. Next to the center was a huge sheep ranch.

One day a sheep rancher in the area was telling us about the birth of some lambs. As he was explaining some of the problems of his business, he told us something that was so horrible I could not get it out of my mind. At lambing time, huge crows fly into the paddock and perch on the backs of the mother sheep. When a lamb is born, the crows hop down and peck out the eyes and tongue of the poor little helpless baby lamb.

When I heard this sad story, I almost became ill. It was almost too much for me. The thought of those newborn lambs being so viciously attacked devastated me. The cruelty of the attackers was so great it was hard to imagine. The helpless condition of the lamb was heartbreaking.

As I reflected on the predicament of newborn lambs, I made application to the spiritual vulnerability of newborn babes in Christ. Isn't it true that the devil is cruel, merciless, and determined to destroy the effectiveness of all the saints? Satan wants to rob us of our spiritual vision for the needs of the world and to silence our voices as we attempt to share the gospel. Some of his most vicious attacks are leveled at new Christians. He will do all within his power to destroy their opportunities for growth and development into mature, fruitful, dedicated disciples.

It is your task and mine to ward off Satan and to provide protection, nourishment, and care to disciples through the perils of spiritual infancy and the temptations of spiritual youth. We are reminded of the apostle Peter's warning: "Be sober, be vigilant; because your adversary the devil, as a roaring lion, walketh about, seeking whom he may devour" (1 Peter 5:8). Be sober! Be wide awake! Be ready always for vicious spiritual opposition. The devil is not simply trying to disturb us or frighten us. He is out to *devour* us.

In the midst of an extremely dangerous situation—which we can oftentimes do nothing about—the devil *does* stalk us. But we can be victorious over his attack. James lays out our strategy very clearly: "Submit yourselves therefore to God. Resist the devil, and he will flee from you" (James 4:7). Here is a two-point program. Submit yourselves to God; take your place under His Lordship, obey His Word, and do His will. Secondly, withstand the devil's attack. It will be a tough fight, but victory is assured. He will eventually flee.

But the new babe knows nothing of the principles of spiritual warfare and the guaranteed victory. It is up to you and me to lead young Christians along the path of growth and discipleship. From the moment of their spiritual birth onward, they need the help and guidance of those of us who have been over the path ourselves. They need to get their roots down into Christ, becoming grounded in the faith.

In 1981 I received a letter from a young man named Rick who had attended a conference where I had preached. He shared some insights that are well worth passing along:

As Christians we are witnesses for Christ. The thing I have to ask myself is, "What kind of a witness do I want to be?" If a radio transmitter does not have a well-grounded antenna, it can't put out a good signal—the power gets lost. If I'm not well-grounded in the Word of God, His Bible, I'll be a weak witness.

I've met some Christians who witness for Christ with a sense of weakness. Everything they say comes out weak. They put out a bad signal because they are not well grounded in the Bible. They even distort the message with their own personal beliefs because they haven't been grounded.

Every time a strong wind blows down a building, I have to suspect that it was not tied well to its foundation. I'm involved with a discipleship program at my church so that I can be sure that I'm well secured to the foundation of God's Word. I want to be ready when Satan sends his worst winds my way.

I thank God for the church I belong to. Also I thank Him for Pastor Hunter.

The winds in this part of Ohio blow mighty strong sometimes. Thank God that he built me a foundation that I can secure myself to for the rest of my life.

The apostle Paul was very direct in his comments on this point: "As ye have therefore received Christ Jesus the Lord, so walk ye in him: rooted and built up in him, and stablished in the faith, as ye have been taught, abounding therein with thanksgiving" (Colossians 2:6-7). The Colossians had received Christ Jesus and had come under His Lordship, but Paul was not satisfied with that. He knew there was more. He spoke to these Colossian believers about their "walk," their progress in the Christian life. And he spoke to them about becoming grounded, rooted, established in the faith. Then, of course, they could begin to build upon that firm foundation, to grow and develop into solid disciples. But everything must come in proper order. First the foundation, then the growth in grace.

Last summer I was in the South Pacific island of Tonga on a preaching tour. A hurricane had recently swept through the area with devastating results. Many buildings had been leveled. Even stone walls had been blown down. We had just come from Fiji, which had experienced the same hurricane but with far less serious results. Why? Because Fiji has a building code, Tonga does not. With no building code, a person can put up anything, but it doesn't last very long. The South Pacific is known for its periodic hurricanes. When they come, many of the buildings go. That's what Paul was trying to get across to the church in Colosse. His comments in Colossians 2:6-7 are his basic building code, giving instructions on how to get started right in the Christian life. As Rick put it in his letter, *tied well to the foundation.*

The laborer is the key to this stabilization process. He is the one who has committed himself to the harvest. He sows *and* reaps. He not only gets the seed into the ground, the hay in the barn, the corn in the crib, the wheat in the granary. He is also responsible for what happens to the crop. The laborer sees himself as a spiritual parent to the new babe in Christ. He feels a responsibility to help the new Christian in four primary areas.

The first area is to help the babe get established in fellowship with the people of God. The new Christian needs to get settled in a good church where he feels welcomed and at home. As he hears God's Word preached and gets to know his brothers and sisters in Christ, he will gradually get oriented to his new life. I recall how helpful it was for me to get to know older Christians and to get invited into their homes. I watched them in their relationships with their children, friends, neighbors, and fellow Christians. It was truly an eye-opener. Everything was so totally different from what I was used to. I was ushered into God's kingdom in such a loving, nurturing way. But without a proper initial orientation, a person could easily become confused and insecure.

At the International Conference for Itinerant Evangelists in Amsterdam in '83, there was an initial orientation to acquaint the speakers with the meeting complex where the plenary sessions and workshops were to be held. Because I missed the orientation, I found it very difficult to know where to go for the various meetings. But although I had not gotten the overall picture at the beginning, I did pick it up bit by bit as the days progressed. In the same way, one of the best methods for a new babe to get a look at the big picture in his newfound faith is to gear in with the household of faith, gradually learning from his fellow Christians.

In addition to all the advantages that come from getting involved in a good church, there are a few basic steps a fresh convert should take to establish fellowship with the Lord. Bible reading is a must, as is Bible study and Scripture memory. Learning to meet the Lord morning by morning in prayer is likewise essential. These fundamentals take time to get established. There are often setbacks and distractions, but the laborer must exercise extreme patience, acceptance, and love.

I recall a young man I was helping in these basics of the faith who at first showed keen interest but soon began to lag. After a little searching, I discovered the reason. A new girl had come into his life who had little or no interest in maintaining any sort of regular fellowship with the Lord. They went out on dates regularly and stayed out late. The guy's morning prayer and Bible reading ceased. He was too tired. His Bible study and Scripture memory became extremely sporadic. Why? His mind was on other things. But through it all he and I remained fast friends.

One day he came to me and told me that he thought he was on the wrong track. He felt that his girlfriend was taking too much of his time and that he should probably cool the relationship. But he had mixed emotions. He really liked being with her.

"LeRoy," he said, "her lips are like honey!" But soon she became interested in another guy and the problem was solved. Setbacks and distractions are a normal part of the discipling process. Love, understanding, acceptance, and patience must be a normal part of it as well.

Second, a new Christian needs help to develop a deep, abiding faith in God. Only then will the person be able to make it through life with a tranquil spirit and a peaceful mind. When it begins to dawn on him that God is truly in control and can be trusted, the peace of God that passes all understanding will guard his heart and mind in Christ.

In the summer of 1982, my wife and I were in Semarang, a city in northern Java. While we were there I saw something that brought this truth about faith home to me quite forcibly. The traffic was horrendous—huge trucks careening through the streets, cars racing around as if they were participants in the Grand Prix, and souped-up motorcycles driven by young daredevils who seemed to care nothing about life or death. What a display!

But the thing that impressed me most were the young ladies sitting sidesaddle behind the young men who were driving what seemed to me to be two-wheel death traps. These young ladies sat there totally unconcerned. Some were reading a book. Others were doing their nails. I was flabbergasted. But the reason for their calm was their absolute faith in the one up front. They knew their young men and trusted them to make it to their destination. The laborer must do all he can to help the new Christian develop that kind of faith in God—confidence in the One "up front."

The third primary area of development for new believers is unconditional surrender to Jesus Christ as the Lord of life and a commitment to do His will. A laborer must communicate that deep level of commitment to the fledglings of the faith. This concept is driven home well in Mark 8:34-37:

> And when he had called the people unto him with his disciples also, he said unto them, Whosoever will come after me, let him deny himself, and take up his cross, and follow me. For whosoever will save his life shall lose it; but whosoever shall lose his life for my sake and the gospel's, the same shall save it. For what shall it profit a man, if he shall gain the whole world, and lose his own soul? Or what shall a man give in exchange for his soul?

This is a message Jesus wanted everyone to hear. He called together His disciples and some other people who were close by. Then He stated three principles of commitment basic to everyone interested in following Him.

You must deny self. The idea is to refuse to associate with, to have no companionship with. Jesus calls us to have no companionship with our fallen nature. Saying yes to Him means saying no to self. If you went up to a total stranger in the shopping mall and said, "Okay, from now on you and I are through. I'm going to have nothing to do with you anymore!" the person would say, "Big deal! We've never had anything to do with each other anyhow, so it makes no difference to me." But if you said it to a close friend, it would mean something. That's what's behind Jesus' teaching here. We must remove *self*, that person who has meant so much to us in the past. We should give up the life of self-interests, self-gratification, self-gain, and self-glory. Paul put it this way: "For the love of Christ constraineth us; because we thus judge, that if one died for all, then were all dead: And that he died for all, that they which live should not henceforth live unto themselves, but unto him which died for them, and rose again" (2 Corinthians 5:14-15).

You must take up your cross. When you see a person carrying something you can often tell where he is going. For instance, if I see the neighbors leaving the house carrying skis, poles, and ski boots, I know they are going to the slopes. If I see them leaving the house carrying blankets, thermos bottles, and a pennant that says "Go Broncos," I know they are going to a football game. In New Testament times, when people saw a man carrying a cross they knew he was going to his death. Carrying a cross means a willingness to suffer. Jesus Himself suffered on our behalf. The apostle Paul said, "God forbid that I should glory, save in the cross of our Lord Jesus Christ, by whom the world is crucified unto me, and I unto the world" (Galatians 6:14).

You must "follow Him." This has to do with our daily walk—a "walk in newness of life" (Romans 6:4). If a person decides to start this journey, there are a few things he must do.

(1) Select the means of travel. For this journey there is only *one:* "We walk by faith."

(2) Decide the route. Christ is the way. "As ye have therefore received Christ Jesus the Lord, so walk ye in him" (Colossians 2:6).

(3) Decide what to take. For this journey there is only one thing: the cross.

(4) Say goodbye to self. Determine to live for the Lord, not for yourself. Self will no doubt whine and plead. But for this journey, which lasts an eternity, there is only room for one driver: Jesus.

Thus far we've seen three basic areas of spiritual life that the budding disciple needs to develop: fellowship with God, faith in God, and surrender to God. The fourth area is service for God. As the growing disciple matures, the laborer must begin to plant seeds of service in his mind, helping him lift up his eyes to see the harvest field, the needs, and the opportunities for witness where he works, lives, plays—wherever. Let's say he begins to develop a desire to see his friends come to Christ. There are a few questions the laborer can ask the new disciple that will strip away some of the confusion and clarify some basic issues: "What kind of training do you need in order to be an effective witness and to help other Christians grow?" "What price are you willing to pay to get this training?"

You as the laborer need to get a commitment from the disciple and then go to work. Help him memorize some key Scripture passages that contain the gospel. Ask him to make up a prayer list of unsaved friends and then get him praying for them. Offer to go to lunch with him and one of his unsaved buddies just to be there with moral support and a brief witness if the opportunity arises. When the disciple gets a taste of real ministry, the Spirit of God can use that to develop some habits that will last a lifetime.

What is the work of a laborer? Paul stated it succinctly and clearly: "[Christ] . . . whom we preach, warning every man, and teaching every man in all wisdom; that we may present every man perfect in Christ Jesus: whereunto I also labour, striving according to his working, which worketh in me mightily" (Colossians 1:28-29). *Warning every man:* That's evangelism. But it doesn't stop there. When people respond to the call of the gospel, a new process begins—*teaching* them in order to help them come to maturity. Hard work? You bet! But nothing is more rewarding than being a laborer in the harvest. "That is what I am working and struggling at, with all the strength that God puts into me" (Colossians 1:29, PH).

CHAPTER FIVE

PRAYER: A LIVING MIRACLE

I was always fascinated to look into my dad's tool chest. He was a master carpenter. His tools were always well kept, each in its place, the best that money could buy. And woe to the person who mistreated one of them, lost one, or used one to do something for which it was not designed. My dad relied on his tools and he constantly made sure each one of them was well taken care of.

The spiritually qualified laborer has certain tools or resources that he relies on and uses in his efforts to win the lost and edify growing Christians. Now we're going to lift the lid and look into his toolbox. Dawson Trotman, the founder of The Navigators, used to tell us that there are seven basic tools for helping others.

One of the most special tools in the disciplemaking ministry is prayer. Daws never looked at prayer as an end in itself. He did not consider prayer a means of self-gratification that would transport him into a state of rapture and ecstasy. He had no desire to be transported into some mystical disengagement from the real world and its real needs. As a genuine prayer warrior, Daws would tell us, "In helping others, if you start with prayer you start with God, and when you start with God you start right."

First of all, through prayer God can reveal what Daws used to call "impediments to growth and usefulness." We are often blind to these stumbling blocks. We can't see the telephone pole in our own eye nearly as clearly as we can see the sliver in the eye of our brother. For me, the prayer of David is classic and to the point: "Search me, O God, and know my heart: try me, and know my thoughts: and see if there be any wicked way in me, and lead me in the way everlasting" (Psalm 139:23-24). A laborer needs to keep growing, but if there are parts of our life that are displeasing to God, then our growth is stunted.

Second, beseech God to help you win the confidence and friendship of the unsaved. In 1957 I went calling each week with one of the pastors of the Dundee Presbyterian Church in Omaha, Nebraska. One afternoon we called at the home of a businessman who was a rough, tough character. Gordon had met the man before and warned me that we might be in for a hard time.

The man came to the door, invited us in, and we began our visit over a cup of coffee. In response to one of his questions I made reference to a book I had read, mentioning how much the book had meant to me and the tremendous esteem and respect I held for the author. This callous businessman seemed surprised. He took me into his study and showed me that very book. He said this book had helped him tremendously, too, and was frankly surprised that someone like myself who was in "religious work" would be aware of such things.

Subsequent to this conversation, he and I became fast friends and to this day—over a period of more than twenty-five years—I have occasional contact with the family. But—best of all—he and most of his family came to know the Lord. The laborer must be diligent to follow Paul's admonition to Timothy to "do the work of an evangelist" (2 Timothy 4:5).

Here is an interesting sidelight to that story. Before

Gordon and I rang the doorbell of that home, I prayed briefly and earnestly that God would cause something to happen during our conversation that would enable me to win the man's onfidence and friendship, influencing him to eventually come to Christ. God answered my prayer.

Third, prayer will help you discover the real needs of a growing Christian and what you can do to help him meet those needs. Pray earnestly for the person. Ask the Lord for discernment. Pray with the person. Often the person will begin to share his heart with the Lord, and through those times of prayer together you will learn what battles he is fighting, what concerns he has, and what problems he is facing in his walk with the Lord. Your ministry in his life will scratch where he really itches.

It is true that we learn by association. This fact is the basis for the apprentice system, through which many of our experts in the building trade learn their remarkable skills. As we spend time in prayer in the presence of the Lord, we become more and more like Him. Paul put it this way: "But we all, with open face beholding as in a glass the glory of the Lord, are changed into the same image from glory to glory, even as by the Spirit of the Lord" (2 Corinthians 3:18).

What a tremendous truth! The secret is to *abide in Christ.*

A fourth reason to pray, therefore, is to become more and more like Christ as we fellowship with Him. For a laborer, one of the most important qualities to develop is Christ's "common touch"—His rapport with the common people. If you and I are to be effective laborers in the vast harvest fields of the world, we must have this common touch with the common people. Christ went to those humble enough to welcome His authoritative Word and His transforming presence.

We will never make much of an impact for Christ if we are

unwilling and unable to communicate spiritual truths to the masses. Jesus communicated openly and effectively. "The common people heard him gladly" (Mark 12:37).

Kenneth Latourette concluded that one of the primary reasons for Christianity's success was that the ministry was taken to the common people, who in turn became the primary means of propagating the gospel.

> The chief agents of the expansion of Christianity appear not to have been those who made it a profession or a major part of their occupation but men and women who earned their livelihood in some purely secular manner and spoke of their faith to those whom they met in the natural fashion, workers in coal, leather, fullers and uneducated persons.

Live in a close abiding fellowship with Christ and let Him live His life through you. He still wants to bring the common people His transforming presence and authoritative Word. This is one of the master keys to that much discussed "cross-cultural ministry."

If anyone ever ministered in a cross-cultural context, it was Jesus. He left His heavenly home, a place of purity and holiness, and came to this polluted, sinful, filthy world to walk among the likes of us. Did He communicate? Yes. Did He communicate to the heart? Yes. Did He get close to the people? Yes. As we reflect on His life and ministry it would seem logical that the most important thing laborers who are called to be cross-cultural missionaries can do is to let Him do it still. Abide in Him. Spend much time in prayer. Minister in the power and fullness of the Holy Spirit. Allow the Spirit of Christ to use you as a channel through which Christ can continue His ministry today.

Does this mean that cross-cultural laborers shouldn't make an effort to understand the times, the culture, or the language? No, of course not. It is merely a matter of priority and trust. Even though they do these things, they must never place their confidence in them. Our confidence is in God. He is the author of our faith, our life, our ministry. The abiding life *will* bear lasting fruit. Jesus said, "I am the vine, ye are the branches: he that abideth in me, and I in him, the same bringeth forth much fruit: for without me ye can do nothing" (John 15:5). This is the secret of an effective ministry with a Christ-like common touch.

Spending time with Christ will keep the laborer on target. This is a fifth benefit that comes to the laborer who prays.

A book that I have read and reread over the years is *Lectures on Preaching* by Phillips Brooks. In the chapter entitled "A Preacher in His Work," he speaks to this matter of keeping our priorities straight and keeping on target. He writes, "Beware of hobbies. Fasten yourself to the center of your ministry, not to some point on its circumference. The circumference must move when the center moves." Good advice. Tangents can be interesting, but we must not live or minister out there.

One laborer I talked to was obsessed with getting a certain kind of music taken off a local radio station. Fair enough. I don't like that kind of music either. The problem was, however, that the man seemed to have lost his interest in soul winning.

Not long ago I had some conversations with a laborer who was on a campaign to promote the idea that drinking wine, beer, and hard liquor is scripturally permitted. He was all taken up with it. The emphasis of his life and ministry had shifted. He was out on the end of a very shaky tangent and I was afraid he was heading for a fall.

A pastor told me recently about a man in his congregation who seems bent on stamping out the Sunday school. This person does not believe in the validity of Sunday school and has made it his all-consuming mission to get rid of it. He is off on a tangent, spending his time and energies on the wrong track, heading in the wrong direction.

A few days ago I talked to a young man who believes the Church should do more to aid political refugees. He spoke of a whole group of people who were being harassed by the government. These people needed help and the Church should get involved. But more than that, he said that it should become the main business of the Church. Most of its resources and time should be spent solving this very knotty problem.

As I heard him out over lunch I was convinced I was listening to a man whose emphasis was off center. The main business of the Church is the Great Commission—winning the lost and edifying the saved. Admittedly, many other matters can in themselves be good, but they must never become the primary focus. I reminded my friend over lunch that Jesus made no effort at planned social revolution or the restructuring of society, but majored on winning individuals. Jesus said of Himself, "The Son of man is come to seek and to save that which was lost" (Luke 19:10).

If you and I want to live our lives at the center, we could do nothing better than spend hours in fellowship with Christ, learning from the One who constantly did what pleased the Father. I'm sure this was the primary reason for the central focus in the life of the apostle Paul. Although he had a profound effect on establishing what the Church believes and made a tremendous contribution to the literature of the faith, he was first and foremost a laborer and only incidentally a theologian and author.

When Daws Trotman had a group of us budding laborers as an audience, he would spend much time challenging us to pray. One day he told us, "When you pray, believe the unbelievable. Make a project list of the impossible things you want God to do." At the top of my list was the desire to be a good witness for Christ. I put two verses at the top of my personal prayer list and prayed over them daily. One was Proverbs 18:24: "A man that hath friends must shew himself friendly: and there is a friend that sticketh closer than a brother."

I had a job at the time loading trucks for Sears, Roebuck. The guys I worked with were not at all interested in the Christian message. I knew that if I were going to win them, I must first make friends with them. Then we could talk and I could share Christ with them in an unhurried, personal way. The other verse was Proverbs 17:22: "A merry heart doeth good like a medicine: but a broken spirit drieth the bones." I figured that if God would help me maintain a friendly attitude and cheery spirit on the job, then He could use me to build a bridge to reach these men with the gospel.

At the time, I didn't think I could do it. But God did it. I got close to those guys and witnessed to them. Then the unbelievable happened! Some of them came to Christ. And the wife of one of the guys came to Christ. With this experience as a beginning, I was motivated to pray for greater and mightier results. I soon learned the privilege and power of prayer. Daws encouraged us to pray for each other. One day he said, "I feel sorry for a person who has many admirers and few intercessors."

My wife and I once had the privilege of visiting Kelepi and Finamoa Mailaui on the island of Tonga in the South Pacific. Kelepi and Fina were both reached for Christ while attending a university in New Zealand. Today they are fruitful laborers back in their home town of Nuku'alofa, the capital of Tonga's 360 islands.

One day they took us on a sightseeing tour of the island. As we went past the Manamo'ui race course, they mentioned that the name Manamo'ui means "living miracle." I looked at the race track as we drove by, and I thought, "No, this race course is not a living miracle. *Prayer* is a living miracle." Through prayer we bring to bear on this world the heart and hand of the living God. Through prayer the lost are brought home. Through prayer the new babe in Christ is helped along on his pilgrimage of faith and is established in his walk with the Lord. Through prayer laborers are thrust forth into the harvest field. Through prayer we can share with God our personal problems and concerns, receiving the light and strength we need for the daily round and common task. Prayer: a living miracle indeed!

CHAPTER SIX

THE WORD OF POWER

In India there are many religious people. Some of the so-called holy men there go about trying to find God by tapping on rocks and trees, whispering, "Are You there? Are You there? Are You there?" The rocks and trees never seem to answer.

But there *are* answers for people seeking God. If only there were enough people to provide these answers. If only these Indian God-seekers could have a conversation with a laborer. For a Christian harvest worker has the best possible tool in his bag for delivering God's answers to the spiritually hungry and perplexed: *The Bible*. The effective laborer points to the Scriptures, of which Jesus Himself said, "They testify of me."

The laborer knows that the Bible is in a class by itself. It is the only book Jesus ever referred to as a source of authority. Although there were huge libraries in existence at that time, Jesus did not quote from the writings of Plato, Aristotle, and Cicero. He was not ignorant of the existence of other books. Why, then, did He make reference to this one book alone? He was showing us that the Bible is unique. All else—a communication from man. The Bible—a communication from God.

Jesus on occasion admonished people for their lack of understanding of the Scriptures. He wanted people to understand *and* to put into practice God's will for man. In one sense the Bible is *God's* book, for He is the source of its truth. But in another sense it is *our* book, for we are the ones who need to apply it.

We are likewise the ones who need to bring the message of God's power to a rebellious planet.

During the period of time in our nation's recent history of campus riots and rebellion, I did a lot of preaching at various colleges and universities. I had a particular experience at the University of Colorado in Boulder that I will never forget. There was a class that met weekly to discuss current events. It was filled with young revolutionaries and radicals. Two students in that class were Christians. One had a huge shock of very curly red hair. The other was a young man who had been completely delivered from hard drugs.

Shortly after their conversion, these two young Christians went to the professor and asked, "Why is it we have had every sort of fanatic come as a guest lecturer to this class, but we've never had a *religious* fanatic? Isn't it about time we had one of those?" The professor said he thought it was a good idea, so he asked them if they knew of one. "Yes," they said, and they called me.

I accepted the invitation. The night before the presentation to the class, I drove from Colorado Springs to Boulder and checked into a motel. As the hours wore on, I began to get nervous. What had I gotten myself into? I called one of the young converts and said, "Tell me again now, what is it you want me to do?" His answer was classic. "What do I want you to do?!! Do your *thing,* man!" Of course! Why didn't I think of that?

So, the next morning I went to the class along with Dean Truog, our local Navigator representative. After Dean's testimony, I gave the gospel as pure and straight as I knew how. Then I opened it up for questions. The place turned into a madhouse, a riot, total bedlam. They were shouting questions, screaming insults and abuses, questioning everything I said. But through the twenty-five minutes of questions, the Lord poured forth His amazing grace, enabling me to answer every question from the Scriptures.

At last the bell rang, indicating that the class was over. At that point an incredible thing happened: They began to applaud. Loudly! And they kept it up. I stood there not knowing exactly how to respond. I smiled. I put my hands in my pockets. I took my hands out of my pockets. I stood on one foot, then the other. And they kept applauding.

As the applause died down and the students began to file out of the room, a young man with long hair, a fringed leather jacket, and a pair of grubby jeans made a beeline to the podium. As he leaped up on the platform, I thought, "Good grief, he's going to hit me!" Instead, he stuck out his hand and said, "I've come up here to do two things. First, to apologize for my behavior this morning, and second, to thank you for coming. Although we shouted and screamed and treated you disrespectfully, it's obvious that you have the answers we need." I said there was no need to apologize and then I thanked him.

Then I went with Dean to the college bookstore to browse around. I've learned that if you want to know what college students are thinking, look to see what they are reading. As we turned to go down one of the aisles, we met the professor of the class. He stopped us, shook hands, and said, "That has *never* happened before! That was amazing! The class has *never* applauded a guest lecturer like they did this morning. It was unbelievable!" I smiled, held up my Bible, and said, "Sir, perhaps you've never had one of these in class before."

It's true, isn't it? The Bible is in a class all by itself. It is worthy of applause. It was Jesus' constant point of reference when He spoke to the people. Many times He would introduce a statement with the words, "Have ye not read . . .?" For example: "But as touching the resurrection of the dead, have ye not read that which was spoken unto you by God, saying, I am the God of Abraham, and the God of Isaac, and the God of Jacob? God is not the God of the dead, but of the living" (Matthew 22:31-32). "He said unto them, Have ye not read what David did, when he was an hungered, and they that were with him . . .?" (Matthew 12:3).

Jesus emphasized the truths of Scripture in order to teach the basics of ministry. The diligent laborer studies the Scriptures so that he will be able to document his own teachings and beliefs. He does as Jesus did. He sticks with the book that is in a class all its own. Moreover, the laborer lives and ministers under the authority of God's Word. He takes seriously the question of Jesus: "Why call ye me, Lord, Lord, and do not the things which I say?" (Luke 6:46).

For many people, what is *right* is determined by what feels good. Their bottom line is what *feels* right. But a laborer is committed to a different principle entirely. What the *Scriptures* teach is right. He is under the sole authority of God's Word. Furthermore, he is committed to helping those to whom he is ministering to come to that place in *their* lives as well. Remember: believing in the inspiration of Scripture has to do with the mind, but being under the authority of Scripture has to do with the will. We should live by the Word of God.

Where did God first give the revelation of His Word? The answer: Palestine, that narrow little strip of land through which the ancient people of three continents traveled: Asia, Africa, and Europe. This fact of biblical history is significant. For this small ridge of land was the geographical center of many civilizations. Because the caravans of traders and merchants constantly roamed back and forth through Palestine, ancient emperors coveted its control.

I believe there is a great lesson here: The Bible is not just for some isolated people but for the mainstream of humanity. It is God's desire that this book be at the heart, the very center of the lives of men and women in every corner of the globe, governing the activities of societies and nations.

But how is this worldwide labor to be done? By *laborers*, of course. Jesus wants harvest workers who are submitted to the authority of the Word, who realize its unique power and who are committed to spreading its message to the harassed and helpless.

A harvest worker has absolute confidence in the power of the Word. He remembers God's question: "Is not my word like as a fire? saith the Lord; and like a hammer that breaketh the rock in pieces?" (Jeremiah 23:29). The Holy Spirit uses the Word to burn out the filth and impurities in our lives, breaking down the walls of resistance we have constructed against Him. But we are often estranged from the power of God's Word. Indeed, there is a lot of fuzzy thinking abroad about just what the power of the Word means.

Some months ago I was on an airplane in the same row with a very nervous young woman. "What kind of airplane is this?" she asked. I answered her question. "Oh no!" she said. "I would not have gotten aboard if I had known that! I never ride in this kind of airplane. It isn't safe!" I assured her that the airplane was perfectly safe, and tried to get her to relax. During the flight she bit her nails, perspired, and drank too much liquor. Meanwhile, I sat there calmly reading my Bible. As we were landing she pointed to my Bible and said, "That's the reason why we weren't all killed." Apparently she looked on the Bible as some sort of magic charm.

I remember Johnny Ating from the jungles of Malaysia telling us about giving a Bible to the natives, who eventually came to use it as a charm to ward off evil spirits. Most people recognize the Bible as something special, something different. Indeed, the Bible is powerful because it is the Word of our almighty, all-powerful God. But at times people look at the book itself as something to be feared and idolized.

One evening we were having an evangelistic dinner in the student union building of the University of Northern Arizona. To get back to our room, we had to walk through the main dining room of the cafeteria. I was walking along when two young women sitting in one of the booths spotted my Bible. One of them asked the other in a frightened voice, "What is *that* doing in here?" The other leaped to her feet and said, "I don't know, but I'm getting out of here!" Together they ran for the nearest exit. Just the sight of the Bible struck terror in their hearts.

The Bible carries God's authority in its message. Often we waste so much of our own physical energy and brainpower trying to persuade others without giving God a chance to move them with His own logic and power. Rather than trying to persuade people solely by our own words, we should give them God's Word and let the power of that Word do its work. When Jesus spoke, the people "were astonished at his doctrine: for his word was with power" (Luke 4:32). That same Word still carries with it that same power.

There is an interesting illustration of this phenomenon in the ministry of Jesus just after His resurrection. His followers had seen His nail-pierced hands and feet—but that was not sufficient, so He also showed them the Word: "And he said unto them, These are the words which I spake unto you, while I was yet with you, that all things must be fulfilled, which were written in the law of Moses, and in the prophets, and in the psalms, concerning me. Then opened he their understanding, that they might understand the scriptures" (Luke 24:44-45). Jesus wanted the testimony and witness of His followers to be based on the impact of the Scriptures.

All those people who want to find God—whether in India, on a college campus, or in a jet high above the earth—can find Him in His guidebook, His Word. The book itself is not possessed by a magical charm, and yet it does proclaim a Word of power—a message that can transform the course of one's life. Those who labor for the Author of Scripture are the *ministers* of this powerful Word (Luke 1:2).

CHAPTER SEVEN

THE PERSONAL TOUCH

What was it like to be with Jesus, to be able to observe Him in action day after day? Several men had the privilege of being with Him on a regular basis for three years. One of these men, the apostle John, described that special daily contact with a sense of awe and wonder:

> That which was from the beginning, which we have heard, which we have seen with our eyes, which we have looked upon, and our hands have handled, of the Word of life . . . that which we have seen and heard declare we unto you, that ye also may have fellowship with us: and truly our fellowship is with the Father, and with his Son Jesus Christ. (1 John 1:1, 3)

These words of John contain a vital laboring principle: Our fellowship with God is closely linked with our fellowship with other believers.

Jesus talked with His disciples, ate with them, traveled with them, and spiritually nurtured them for three years. It was a special kind of fellowship. But it was not so unique that it has no parallels. Picture in your mind the kind of learning relationship the young Joshua had with the seasoned Moses. Think of what great lessons Elisha learned from Elijah. Consider also the spiritual bond that developed through the years between Timothy and the wise apostle Paul.

Spending time with someone makes all the difference. Jesus "ordained twelve, that they should be *with him,* and that he might send them forth to preach" (Mark 3:14). We can learn much about the Lord by spending time with His representatives, His laborers. The Navigators refer to this as the "with Him" principle.

What ever happened to this kind of close personal bond? Is the "with Him" principle outdated? Is it no longer valid?

I experienced this principle in action when I was a new Christian at Northwestern College in Minnesota. Don Rosenberger, the local Navigator representative, occasionally took me with him when he went to speak in a church or at a rally. As we were driving to some nearby town, Don would be applying this principle.

Usually it was just the two of us in the car. We would talk about everything—spiritual things, ordinary things, current events, the future. Mostly we just got to know each other. It was a truly enjoyable experience. But I didn't realize at the time that Don was applying a tremendously powerful principle that God was using to shape my life. Through his love and concern for me, Don was teaching me indirectly about Jesus. By being with him, I was learning about Him.

Like Timothy reminiscing about his experiences with Paul, I look back on those times with Don with great fondness and gratitude. This kind of special relationship increases the depth and effectiveness of the ministry of the laborer. Let him take the young disciple to a ball game, to the ski slopes, to a concert, to picnics and backyard barbecues—anywhere and everywhere. Through it all, the life touch will be there. Through it all, the things that are more caught than taught will be implanted in the life.

Early in my years of heading up the Navigator ministry in the Midwest, God spoke to me from Acts 20:4: "And there accompanied him into Asia Sopater of Berea; and of the Thessalonians, Aristarchus and Secundus; and Gaius of Derbe, and Timotheus; and of Asia, Tychicus and Trophimus." What a picture! Young laborers in training—living, walking, suffering, ministering with the apostle Paul.

"He that walketh with wise men shall be wise: but a companion of fools shall be destroyed" (Proverbs 13:20). Paul chose this simple plan of training young men by bringing them with him on the road of life. Why didn't Paul start a school for the training of laborers? Was it because he didn't have enough contacts? Nonsense! There would have been a line a mile long waiting to get in. Was it because he didn't have the academic qualifications. Nonsense! Paul was one of the few if not the only one who did. Then why did he choose this method? The answer is abundantly clear and simple. Paul knew he could not improve on the method of Jesus Christ. He knew what Jesus had done and he followed it as closely as he knew how.

In 1952 Virginia and I were asked by Dawson Trotman to go to Seattle to be involved in the ministry there. We moved into the Nav home where Gordon Donaldson, the local Nav representative and his wife, Chris, were living. They were both well-grounded Christians, but we were young believers who knew so very little. Although there is no way we can express what that time meant to us, one thing is clear. Some years later when we opened our home to young men and women, the lessons God had taught us in Seattle were precious. And many of those lessons came not from our Bible study time or prayer time together, but from that second cup of coffee around the breakfast table or the time working on the lawn together. Howard Hendricks said that one of the best discipling tools is the dining room table.

Don Rosenberger took me with him because he was concerned for my spiritual growth. He was applying a principle that God had used in his life through Kenny Watters, a fellow Navy chief who led him to Christ in Honolulu shortly after the attack on Pearl Harbor. May God grant you the vision to see the potential in your life for touching the life of someone else for Christ.

Whereas the "with Him" principle is a rather general friendship approach to training, the "one-to-one" principle is usually more structured. Its usefulness is primarily in the training of laborers, but each laborer must make use of it as well in his efforts to help the growing Christian become a mature, dedicated, fruitful disciple. Admittedly, the bulk of his contact with the young Christian may be at a small group level, but he must supplement his group fellowship with periodic one-to-one training and counsel.

Let's say you have four or five young Christians in your church, your Sunday school, or your men's or women's fellowship who are clearly eager to grow. You realize that if they aren't helped and challenged to the maximum of their interest and potential, their growth will be stunted and possibly their interest cooled. But what to do? You can't possibly get with all of them on a one-to-one basis, and maybe you shouldn't. Quite possibly the most effective thing you can do is to get them in a small group Bible study.

First of all, if they are keen on the idea, agree on some ground rules. I have found that it's best to discuss these guidelines with them, rather than throwing your weight around by "laying down the law." Ask them for their opinions: Shall we agree to have our lessons prepared when we come to our Bible study group? Shall we include Scripture memory as part of our study? How many verses per week? Where?"

When you clear the air ahead of time by bringing them

into the decision-making process and letting them help set the standards, you are likely to get a greater degree of cooperation and commitment. Now it's *their* study: they made the rules, so full speed ahead!

My advice is to start with basic topical studies in order to help the young disciples get established in Christian doctrine. There are many good studies designed to help new converts make progress toward becoming mature, dedicated disciples. (I highly recommend the *Design for Discipleship* series and the *Studies in Christian Living* series published by NavPress.)

Some might ask, Why not begin by studying the books of the Bible? My experience would say, *later.* First lay a solid foundation on the various topics that are vital to the inexperienced, growing Christian. *Then* begin to study different books of Scripture. I have found it helpful to do a few shorter books first. It gives the growing Christian a good feeling to know he has completed something. Solomon reminds us that "the desire accomplished is sweet to the soul" (Proverbs 13:19). Philippians, 1 Thessalonians, 1 Timothy, and 2 Timothy are good "starters." After finishing a couple of these, you can then suggest a study of a longer book such as Romans or John. Look upon the question and answer studies as a solid foundation upon which you begin to build the superstructure with the study of various books of the Bible.

If you have your study weekly, you might like to try the early morning hour. For years I have met with men from 6:30 to 7:30 A.M., having breakfast together and then going off to work. It's a great way to start the day. Such an early time does not conflict with other plans and it adds a touch of heartiness to meet in the early hours. Begin with a prayer to commit the time to the Lord. Then check each other on your new Scripture verses to make sure each of you has them word perfect. This takes only a few minutes if you pair up by twos and quote them to each other.

Remember: You are the leader, not the teacher. Ask discussion questions; keep the study moving; and at the end it's often good to give a brief challenge before closing in prayer.

"Okay," you say, "but where does one-to-one time fit into all this?" Simply put, your one-to-one time with these people can be seen in the same way that a medic looks on a soldier who has been wounded. If someone is being attacked by the forces of darkness, if he is having problems with overexertion, divisions, priorities, demotivation, or other serious trials, it's time to get that person aside and help him through it. Apply spiritual first aid. Pray with him; comfort him; encourage him— whatever it takes to keep him going.

As the group continues to meet, it will become evident to you which individuals are the most motivated and eager to learn and grow. These are the ones to whom you want to begin giving personal time. But let them evidence the hunger and desire before you approach them individually. If you move too soon, you could scare them off. However, the eager ones will not continue to be satisfied with just what you can give them during the study time. They will *want* you to share your life with them. That's where the "with Him" principle begins to mesh with a variation of "one-to-one" in the context of your small group. No single method is sufficient in itself to do the job of developing laborers, but many can be valuable. The suggestions I have given are merely illustrative. Use them as they best fit your situation.

In the summer of 1951, Dawson Trotman told of a very discouraging pattern he had observed in the military ministry. Large groups were failing to produce many effective laborers. "Why?" Daws asked. "Because a mother knows how to care for her baby but not how to run an orphanage. First Corinthians 4:15 is why the large groups often fizzle out."

In this Corinthian passage, Paul described the father-son

kind of relationship that takes place in one-to-one. There should be a mature concern on the part of the leader for certain young Christians. But the leader of a large group just can't meet the personal needs of all the group members. Sometimes people get lost in the shuffle. That's why I urge you to learn to use the tool of the small group fellowship, supplemented by periodic times of one-to-one fellowship. And learn also to use the "with Him" principle.

Daws listed eight vital guidelines for leaders to help the new Christian grow.

1. Build in him a life that will glorify God.

2. Build in him a life centered in Christ that is supported by regular prayer, Bible study, witnessing, and fellowship.

3. Get him into contact with other strong Christians.

4. Get him into the right environment.

5. Teach him. "When they were alone, he expounded all things to his disciples" (Mark 4:32).

6. Observe him.

7. Give him experience.

8. Pray with him.

Since each individual is different, you will have to play it by ear in your one-to-one encounters. But one thing comes across loud and clear. We need to do all within our power to help these new ones count for God.

One more vital factor in motivating the growing Christian— meeting his needs and drawing his heart closer to the Lord—is church attendance. It is essential to involve new Christians in the life of the local church. The church is the logical place to get that personal touch that we all need. As I look back now on a period of over thirty years, I have never seen a person do well over the long haul who early on in his walk with God did not get involved in the life of a local church. There may be some, but I have never seen them. It may indeed happen, but it must be a rare event.

There are no doubt many ways to positively influence the life of a new believer. But we must never forget that it is almost impossible for that believer to thrive without the close personal contact of a more experienced Christian who cares about him. As we reflect on the needs of growing Christians, let's be in prayer that God will use us as "wise masterbuilders" in the cause of Christ (1 Corinthians 3:10). For this is the privilege and responsibility of laborers.

CHAPTER EIGHT

THE SPIRIT WHO GUIDES US

Shortly after my family and I moved to Pittsburgh to begin our first assignment with The Navigators, we received a letter from Dawson Trotman. Bill Bright was beginning a campus ministry and had asked Daws for the loan of some men to get it kicked off. He asked if I was interested.

"Yes," I wrote back immediately. "I am keenly interested. I'd like to do it."

A few weeks later Bill came to town to show us the ropes. As he got off the plane, he introduced us to the man he had led to Christ on the flight from Los Angeles. That was an appropriate first exposure to Bill Bright.

Bill stayed with us for three days. During those three days, we did basically two things: pray and evangelize. We spent much time in prayer together claiming the promises of God. And we spent many hours on campus. We held an evangelistic meeting in a fraternity house and we interviewed students on campus. Three people came to Christ as a result of our fraternity meeting: the president of the fraternity, the captain of the swimming team, and the goalie on the soccer team. It was exciting.

As Bill and I talked, I became aware of something that had always been a bit mysterious to me. Bill spoke of the Holy Spirit

69

in far more intimate terms than I had ever heard before. Bill taught us how to conduct meetings in the fraternity, how to interview students regarding their relationship with Christ, and how to function as a gospel team on campus. He taught us so much, but he communicated far more than he taught. His life communicated a passion for souls, a commitment to the Great Commission, an absolute confidence in the power of the gospel, and a reliance on the Word of God. All of these things I understood. But there was one aspect of Bill's life that I didn't fully understand. He had a relationship with the Holy Spirit that was beyond me. And I sensed that this relationship had something to do with his amazing fruitfulness in evangelism.

After Bill left town, I determined to get alone with God and sort out all these things as best I could. I needed a personal word from the Lord regarding this ministry. So I went to the third floor of the home where we were living and spent three weeks alone with God in prayer and in His Word. My objective was twofold. One was to get a confirmation from God directly from His Word on our means of outreach in evangelism. The second was to come to a new understanding of the ministry of the Holy Spirit in and through my life.

I approached the second objective with great care. I didn't want to make a mistake or get on a wrong track. My caution stemmed from something that had happened during my first year as a new Christian at Northwestern College. I had met some keen young men and women whose dedication to Christ and joy in the Lord was an inspiration. During our first semester an evangelist came to one of the local churches with a soul winning and healing ministry. Soul winning I had heard of. But a healing ministry—that was a new one.

One night some of my zealous, joyful classmates went to the meeting. The next morning I noticed something peculiar. One of them who had worn very thick glasses was no longer wearing them. I was told a healing had taken place and that the glasses had been thrown away. But when this person tried to read, she held her book about 5 inches from her eyes, squinted at the page, and read with extreme difficulty. One of my friends who lived in the same dorm with her told me that when she tried to iron her clothing she practically burned her nose because she had to get her head so close to the fabric to see what she was doing. It was plain that she could hardly see. And the credit for it all went to the Holy Spirit.

I was not impressed. I concluded that the girl had been duped. Surely if the Holy Spirit had been at work in her life correcting her eyesight, He would have done a much better job. Some of them who had spoken in tongues for the first time at the meetings tried to get me to go that week, but I declined. It didn't seem to be something that I wanted to get involved with. I had met The Navigators and was involved with them in Bible study, Scripture memory, prayer meetings, rallies, and so on. I decided I would stick with that.

But now here I was, four years after that campus incident, making a concerted effort to study the Scriptures on the person and work of the Holy Spirit and trying to grow in my relationship with Him.

At a Navigator conference a couple of years prior to this, I had heard Dawson Trotman answer a question about why the wheel illustration contained nothing about the Holy Spirit. Daws occasionally referred to the wheel as an illustration of the Christ-centered, Spirit-filled life. And yet there was nothing in the illustration about the Spirit of God. Why was this?

Daws explained that the Spirit is active in each part of the wheel: the Word, prayer, obedience, and witnessing. The hub of the wheel represents Christ, who must be the center of our lives. He is Lord. Daws would remind us that "no man can say that Jesus is the Lord, but by the Holy Ghost" (1 Corinthians 12:3). The Spirit reveals spiritual truth to us as we study the Word. For the Holy Spirit is "the Spirit of truth" (John 14:17).

The effectiveness of prayer is clearly dependent on the Holy Spirit. "Likewise the Spirit also helpeth our infirmities: for we know not what we should pray for as we ought: but the Spirit itself maketh intercession for us with groanings which cannot be uttered. And he that searcheth the hearts knoweth what is the mind of the Spirit, because he maketh intercession for the saints according to the will of God" (Romans 8:26-27).

There are many Scriptures that relate the life of obedience to the Holy Spirit. Paul wrote, "Grieve not the holy Spirit of God, whereby ye are sealed unto the day of redemption" (Ephesians 4:30). I grieve the Holy Spirit by living in disobedience to the Word. Paul likewise told the Thessalonians, "Quench not the Spirit" (1 Thessalonians 5:19). We should never refuse to engage in some service the Lord has for us to do. The Spirit wants to bestow unhindered blessing on our lives. If God speaks to us about some inner sin and we then refuse to deal with it, we grieve the Holy Spirit. If we refuse when He speaks to us about getting involved in some outreach for Christ or some good work in His name, then we quench the operative power of the Spirit in and through our lives. The relationship between the Holy Spirit and a life of obedience is clear-cut.

Acts 1:8 was one of the verses Daws had us memorize early in our growth as disciples: "But ye shall receive power, after that the Holy Ghost is come upon you: and ye shall be witnesses unto me both in Jerusalem, and in all Judaea, and in Samaria, and unto the uttermost part of the earth." Here again we can readily see the relationship between witnessing and the Holy Spirit.

When I had listened to Daws explain how the Holy Spirit was in each part of the wheel illustration, I was satisfied. But during that time in Pittsburgh I was exploring a new dimension of the Spirit's activities. As I studied the Word I became aware of passages of Scripture that spoke of "an anointing," "the power of the Spirit," and being "filled with the Spirit." So I went to work on a fascinating Bible study that God used to change my life.

I discovered that the anointing of the Holy Spirit relates to two aspects of the Christian life. First of all, it signifies a separation unto God for the service He has ordained. The Scriptures speak of "how God anointed Jesus of Nazareth with the Holy Ghost and with power: who went about doing good, and healing all that were oppressed of the devil; for God was with him" (Acts 10:38).

Secondly, the anointing refers to the teaching ministry of the Holy Spirit. "The anointing which ye have received of him abideth in you, and ye need not that any man teach you: but as the same anointing teacheth you of all things, and is truth, and is no lie, and even as it hath taught you, ye shall abide in him" (1 John 2:27). These two things, I concluded, were very practical and vital ministries of the Holy Spirit. I determined that He would be my Teacher as I studied the Word and that He would help me in my witness for Christ.

I then turned my attention to the *power* of the Holy Spirit. When Paul spoke of his witness being in "the power of the Spirit of God" (Romans 15:19), he used a word from which we get our word *dynamite,* the same word he used in Romans 1:16 to call attention to his confidence in the gospel: "For I am not ashamed of the gospel of Christ: for it is the power of God unto salvation to every one that believeth; to the Jew first, and also to the Greek." I saw that it is simply a matter of choice. Would I rely on my own strength or on God's? It is a matter of confidence. There in that third-floor room I determined to place my confidence in God, living in His power rather than in my own.

But there was also a third matter I had to deal with: the *fullness* of the Spirit. I was excited when I read that the apostles "were all filled with the Holy Ghost, and . . . spake the word of God with boldness" (Acts 4:31). It was much on my heart to be the kind of bold witness I had seen in the life of Bill Bright.

But what did it mean to be "filled with the Spirit?" I knew it was important because Paul expressed it as a command: "Be not drunk with wine, wherein is excess; but be filled with the Spirit" (Ephesians 5:18). Then I saw it. The apostles were ministering under the influence and control of the Holy Spirit in the same way a drunk is under the influence and control of the alcohol he has consumed.

As I sat there, I put it all together: I must yield myself completely to God for the ministry He has called me to do. I must trust Him to lead me aright as He teaches me His Word. I must minister in His power, relying completely on Him rather than on my own strength or wisdom. I must yield my life to His control. And if I would follow these commands, I could trust Him to make my life fruitful, a life that would bring glory to Him.

Something happened to me during those three weeks that I spent in that upper room with Christ in prayer and the study of His Word—something that has had a profound effect on my life over the years. For the first time I saw myself as a channel. From now on it would be Christ by His Spirit ministering His gospel *through me,* as Paul said in Romans 15:18. That simple thought was the greatest source of release that I had ever encountered. I no longer carried the burden of results. It was all His. He merely wanted to use me to accomplish His task. When, after three weeks of prayer and searching the Word, I left that room and hit the campus with the gospel, it was with a great sense of expectation, excitement, and support. I could relax and enjoy it. It wasn't my work. It was His. He would lead me day after day.

I went to the campus under His anointing, in His power, and in His fullness, claiming promises from His Word that He had given. God proceeded to fulfill those promises. Consequently, it was clear who got the credit for the results of that ministry. All the glory belonged to the Lord. Those of us who took the gospel to those students were merely channels through whom God condescended to work.

A few years ago I was ministering the Word to some students at the University of Wyoming. One of the questions they raised was about the ministry of the Holy Spirit. They wondered about the relationship between the Holy Spirit and the Lord Jesus Christ. I took them to John 16:14 where Jesus said, speaking of the Holy Spirit, "He shall glorify me: for he shall receive of mine, and shall shew it unto you." Here we have the great overriding ministry of the Holy Spirit: to glorify Christ. He has no interest in drawing attention to Himself.

In 1974 Virginia and I attended an opera in the Great Opera House in Vienna, Austria. There was a man located in a booth up above the third balcony who was operating a spotlight. Throughout the entire opera he kept the spotlight on the central figure of the story as it was acted out on stage. As I sat there in that magnificent building, it occurred to me that this was a picture of the ministry of the Holy Spirit. The central figure in all the universe is Jesus Christ. The Holy Spirit remains in the shadows, His primary task to shine the spotlight of the Word of God on the person of Jesus Christ.

It would do the Spirit a disservice to invite Him down from the shadows to share center stage with Jesus. He would be uncomfortable in that role. His mission is to call attention to Jesus while He Himself remains invisible. He has no interest in someone calling attention to Him. He illuminates the Word so that we can see Jesus.

As I look back now, I can see that Dawson Trotman's constant desire was to keep us Christ-centered—witnessing for Him, living for Him. "To know Christ and to make Him known" was our motto. I thank God for that focus. And I thank God for those three weeks alone with Him, when He took me a step further in my understanding of the ministry of the blessed Spirit of God—the One who perpetually supports us.

CHAPTER NINE

THE PHYSICAL DEMANDS OF SPIRITUAL LABOR

A few weeks ago I was having dinner with my good friend Dr. Noel Lloyd of Seattle, Washington. We were chatting over a leisurely meal in the restaurant of the Bellevue Athletic Club. Noel has been very successful in his profession and has been a dynamic witness for Christ. He is a young man who has already accomplished most of those things that others his age hope to achieve in a lifetime.

As we were discussing the general topic of goal setting, he said, "LeRoy, it seems to me that for a person to accomplish anything in life he needs three things: creativity, energy, and the will to stick with his chosen path. Creativity is needed to figure out what he wants to do to set the course of his life. Then a person needs the energy to do it, and the consistency and will to plug along day by day."

As I look back over my own life, I know he is right. But in the past I have had some deep misconceptions about the second item on his list: the need for physical energy.

My first overseas preaching tour was in 1963. I visited ten countries in six weeks, preaching an average of twice a day. After a week-long staff conference in Baden Baden, Germany, I was taken to Bitburg, Germany to preach at the Servicemen's Center. After a rather hectic and exciting trip in a Volkswagen on a narrow, winding road, we finally arrived. I was tired, but I didn't realize just how tired I really was.

After supper we gathered in the Servicemen's Center with around forty men and women who were stationed at the American Air Force base. I was scheduled to speak on the topic, "What God is Looking for in a Man." After some good rousing hymns and a testimony or two, I was on. I walked to the podium, looked out at the crowd, and said, "Do you know what God is looking for?" Then I just stood there. I knew there had to be dozens of things God was looking for in our lives, but I couldn't think of *one*. I just stood there staring at the crowd. My mind went blank.

After a few minutes of absolute silence, Jack Blanch, the director of the center, walked up to me, shook my hand, and led me through the crowd to my bedroom. He told me to go to bed and get some sleep. Then he dismissed the crowd and the evening of fellowship was ended.

What was my problem? Was it that I didn't know what to do? No, my assignment was clear. Was it a problem of the will? No, I was willing to speak to the crowd. It was simply a problem of running out of energy. I didn't need another meeting. I needed a few good nights of rest.

A similar thing had happened to me some years before when I was a student at Northwestern College. Not only was I carrying a twenty-one-hour course load, which included four hours of New Testament Greek, but I was also loading trucks four hours a day and eight hours on Saturday. My first class was at 7:15 A.M., which meant I had to leave the apartment to catch the streetcar at around 6:30 A.M. In order for me to have breakfast and a morning quiet time, I had to get up at 5:30 A.M. I spent all morning at the school, hurried home, had lunch, went to work, returned home, had supper, and then studied until around midnight. In addition, I was involved in the local

Navigator team, leadership of the youth department in my church, one-to-one discipling of two high school seniors, an evening young people's group, and evening church service. All of these activities devoured my time and energy.

I maintained this schedule for months. Since I was young and vigorous, I thought nothing of it. Then one morning while sitting in History 303, I fell off my chair. I completely passed out. I had simply run out of energy. Some friends took me home and put me to bed, where I stayed for about four days.

When I returned to classes, the school nurse called me into her office to tell me that I had to slow down. But I didn't. On the Iowa farm where I was raised, it was drummed into my head, "Hard work never killed anybody," "The early bird gets the worm," and so on. On the farm there was very little emphasis on taking care of oneself. There didn't need to be. We had plenty of fresh vegetables from our garden. We butchered our own meat and had lots of fresh milk to drink. Furthermore, we went to bed early and worked hard all day.

When we moved to town, I was involved in the usual small town high school sports—baseball, basketball, and track. After graduation from high school, I joined the Marines. During the fighting in the South Pacific in World War II, I was hit in the knee with shrapnel, causing some permanent damage that made it impossible to run. So for years I went without exercise.

During the autumn of 1956, I began to get daily headaches. I asked the Lord to take them away, but nothing happened. I began to worry. What was wrong with me? One day I was talking with Dick Simmons, the local Young Life rep. Dick was a heavyweight wrestler with a keen interest in physical conditioning. He asked me what I did to keep in shape. I told him I did nothing because I could no longer engage in sports. Dick invited me to come down to the local gym to work out. He said he could teach me some exercises that wouldn't hurt my knee. Through this encounter I discovered something that has been tremendously helpful to me over the years, something that has completely changed my life: *We need to take care of our bodies.* Today I am a firm believer in the value of proper diet, regular exercise, and sufficient rest. By the way, the headaches soon left, never to return.

Certainly self-discipline is essential in our physical fitness. But what is the ultimate source of our energy, vitality, and strength? Scripture gives us the answer:

> Hast thou not known? hast thou not heard, that the everlasting God, the Lord, the Creator of the ends of the earth, fainteth not, neither is weary? there is no searching of his understanding. He giveth power to the faint; and to them that have no might he increaseth strength. Even the youths shall faint and be weary, and the young men shall utterly fall: But they that wait upon the Lord shall renew their strength; they shall mount up with wings as eagles; they shall run, and not be weary; and they shall walk, and not faint. (Isaiah 40:28-31)

This passage contains a much needed reminder in a day when health and exercise have practically become a religion in the Western world. Which tennis shoes to buy, which diet plan to follow, which health club to join—these have become important issues for a great number of people.

But the words of the psalmist help us keep our perspective: "God hath spoken once; twice have I heard this; that power belongeth unto God" (Psalm 62:11). The source of all energy, both physical and spiritual, is God. Keeping this in mind prevents us from falling into the trap of placing our confidence in any second cause—in some human invention or scheme, or in something other than God Himself. God, the One who never faints, gives strength to those who do have a tendency to faint. His Word to us is clear: "Fear thou not; for I am with thee: be not dismayed; for I am thy God: I will strengthen thee; yea, I will help thee; yea, I will uphold thee with the right hand of my righteousness" (Isaiah 41:10).

There is an intriguing part of Jacob's blessing on Joseph in which he referred to God as the shepherd and stone of Israel (Genesis 49:24). When a person begins to build his life on the Rock of Ages and comes to realize that the Lord is *his* shepherd, his life takes on new zest and gusto. Fear, guilt, shame, uncertainty, and many other plagues on the mind of modern man take a serious toll on man's physical energy as well. But when God forgives, redeems, and justifies in response to repentance and faith, a whole new life begins. I have seen people who were listless, lifeless, and sapped of strength suddenly come alive physically when they experienced a spiritual new birth.

We are indeed fearfully and wonderfully made. There seems to be a direct connection, amid the complexity of the human being, between the physical and spiritual dimensions. I have seen spiritual energy transmitted to physical energy, and vice versa.

God communicates the daily strength we need through two primary means—the ordinary and the extraordinary. One example of an extraordinary provision of God to His people is found in the promise of Deuteronomy 33:25: "Thy shoes shall be iron and brass; and as thy days, so shall thy strength be." Christian, do you have work to do today that seems a bit beyond you? God can give you strength. Just as He can help you carry an emotional burden or meet a spiritual temptation, so He can provide physical energy sufficient for the day. The psalmist said, "The Lord will give strength unto his people; the Lord will bless his people with peace" (Psalm 29:11).

The Bible refers to the people of God as those who "quenched the violence of fire, escaped the edge of the sword, out of weakness were made strong, waxed valiant in fight, turned to flight the armies of the aliens" (Hebrews 11:34). This is a description of very physical encounters. You and I can expect the same kind of help from the Lord. But the Lord expects certain things from us as well. He has promised to renew the strength of those who *wait* on Him.

As we run the race set before us, we must be constantly "looking unto Jesus." This involves certain basic disciplines such as a consistent intake of the Word through study of the Scriptures, Scripture memory, and unhurried meditation and prayer. Because of Samson's heartfelt prayer, God restored his physical strength that he had lost through sin.

It is abundantly clear that God can give physical strength and energy to His people through supernatural means such as prayer and faith. But it is also clear from the Bible that there are ordinary means as well. A particular incident that took place during the wars of Israel shows this fact clearly. After Jonathan had grown weary from fighting Philistines, he simply scooped up some honey, ate it, and his strength was restored (1 Samuel 14:27-29). All he needed was a bit of nourishment to revive him. God used the honey to raise his blood sugar level until he was energized again for the battle.

The apostle Paul emphasized the ordinary means God uses to help us run the race, keeping us in the spiritual battle:

> Know ye not that they which run in a race run all, but one receiveth the prize? So run, that ye may obtain. And every man that striveth for the mastery is temperate in all things. Now they do it to obtain a corruptible crown; but we an incorruptible. I therefore so run, not as uncertainly; so fight I, not as one that beateth the air: But I keep under my body, and bring it into subjection: lest that by any means, when I have preached to others, I myself should be a castaway. (1 Corinthians 9:24-27)

Paul stated to the Corinthians that he disciplined himself physically like an athlete in strict training. As we reflect on Paul's perspective, we can readily see that maintaining one's body through proper eating habits and regular exercise is an ordinary course by which God keeps us going.

About the same time that Dick Simmons introduced me to a regular exercise program, I met Mrs. Kay Marshall, who had studied nutrition at Iowa State University. She began to explain to me the chemical composition of various foods. I purchased a book that described various foods according to vitamins, minerals, proteins, and so on. That study produced lasting changes and restrictions in my eating habits.

Each of us has unique sleep, rest, and relaxation requirements. We need to learn what physical routine is best for us. We must pace ourselves but not pamper ourselves. Over the years I have seen the importance of using Sunday as a day of spiritual and physical refreshment. Sunday school, morning worship, an afternoon nap, and the evening service are standard fare around our house.

Some years ago I learned the difference between the kind of exercise that works your heart and lungs and the kind that works your muscles. I have tried to include both in my exercise program. Because of the limitations on my left knee, I cannot jog. But I have worked out a routine that the Lord has used to keep me fairly healthy through the years. While I work out I listen to the Bible on cassette tape. It is a very refreshing time.

Serving the Lord in any capacity requires physical strength and endurance. Spiritual labor makes serious physical demands of us. After many years of the right kind of diet, rest, and exercise, I am convinced that God has used these forms of bodily maintenance to keep me going in spite of a tough schedule, some tough problems, and a demanding job. As Christians, we should always keep in mind *God's* perspective on our bodies:

Know ye not that your body is the temple of the Holy Ghost which is in you, which ye have of God, and ye are not your own? For ye are bought with a price: therefore glorify God in your body, and in your spirit, which are God's. (1 Corinthians 6:19-20)

CHAPTER TEN

PRODUCING THOSE WHO REPRODUCE

The need for laborers is great. But where do they come from? Is there something you and I can do to help populate the world with laborers? Yes, of course there is. The primary endeavor is to pray, because in the final analysis laborers come from God.

Prayer was Jesus' amazingly basic solution to the labor shortage (Matthew 9:38). We must not look to man, to methods, to the machinery of slick, clever religious programs, or to the best ideas this world has to offer. Admittedly, books by various secular experts or articles in business and management magazines may stimulate thought and prove helpful, but we must never turn to these for our basic solutions. We must turn to God in prayer and search His Word for His mind on the matter. The starting point for this renaissance of laboring must be the Great Commission.

Jesus came to bring salvation and eternal life to a lost and dying world. In the process He recruited some men to help—men whose lives would be the foundations of countless spiritual generations; men who would multiply their impact on the world by winning and training others, who in turn would repeat the process. Paul put it this way: "The things that thou hast heard of me among many witnesses, the same commit thou to faithful men, who shall be able to teach others also" (2 Timothy 2:2).

God has purposed to develop spiritually qualified laborers through people who have a ministry one step beyond disciplemaking. Their ministry is to multiply the number of those who are disciples in the fullest sense and who disciple others. They know that to do less is to miss completely the spiritual multiplication principle that Paul urged on Timothy (2 Timothy 2:2), thus leading to a dead-end ministry. Daws used to tell us that emotion is no substitute for action, action is no substitute for production, and production is no substitute for reproduction. His focus was on *producing reproducers.*

We have seen that God uses laborers to help converts become disciples. But who does God use to equip the laborer for his task? Paul tells us in Ephesians 4:11-12, "And he gave some, apostles; and some, prophets; and some, evangelists; and some, pastors and teachers; for the perfecting of the saints, for the work of the ministry, for the edifying of the body of Christ." Here Paul cites certain people who equip others to labor. Over the years we Navigators have called them "MDMs" (makers of disciplemakers) and "reproducers." But Paul's description has led us to refer to them simply as *"equippers."* These equippers are themselves laborers whom God uses to equip disciples to become laborers.

There are some spiritual warnings the equipper must keep in mind, for the powers of darkness are definitely out to destroy him and his ministry.

The first warning to the equipper: Do not allow the prospective laborer to develop a passive, unhealthy reliance on you. Rather, keep ever before the budding laborer his personal responsibility to the Lord. His primary responsibilities are to God: consistent fellowship with Christ, diligent study of and obedience to the Word of God, and renewed commitments to the Lordship of Christ. The believer must assume certain responsibilities for his own life. Jude spoke of this when he called on the believer to "earnestly contend for the faith," when he wrote about "*building up yourselves* on your most holy faith," exhorting them to "*keep yourselves* in the love of God" (Jude 3,20,21).

The second warning for the equipper: Do not look at yourself as a ministry technician majoring on ministry skills. Rather, emphasize the qualities of life that God can use to make your apprentice an effective laborer. Jesus taught his men to be servants of all (Mark 10:44). He modeled a compassion for the lost (Matthew 9:36). He emphasized a life of faith (Matthew 21:21-22). He put a priority on love (John 13:34-35). The list of these inner qualities could go on and on. But it is amazing how *little* Jesus spoke to His men on ministry skills. He majored on the man rather than on ministry methods.

The third warning for the equipper: Do not overreact by underrating the value of teaching ministry skills. After all, a laborer in any profession needs to learn his job. A bricklayer is not a good bricklayer simply because he is a loving father and husband. A carpenter is not a good carpenter simply because he has compassion for the homeless. No, the equipper must train the laborers to be good workers in the harvest field. The harvest will be gathered quicker and more efficiently if the laborers know their business.

The fourth warning to the equipper: Avoid the notion that this training can be done in a vacuum. I fell prey to this error in my early days as an equipper, and with disastrous results. I had met a man who was eager to learn. I was certainly eager to share what I had learned, so it appeared to be an ideal situation. So we began to meet for one hour each week in my basement. I had gone to a number of Navigator conferences where I had taken many good notes on such subjects as the importance of the Word, Scripture memory, purity of life, witnessing, follow-up, one-to-one training, and world vision. I went over the notes in my notebook and he wrote them in his. We had *great* times together.

It was a blessing for me to share these concepts and it was a blessing for him to receive them. They were vital, important truths and there was great enthusiasm on both our parts. But that was as far as it went. After I exhausted my notes, he thanked me for all the good information, but since he did not know anyone who wanted to learn these things, he closed his notebook and that was that. I had enriched his store of interesting spiritual truths and he was grateful. But he did not learn to labor. He had notes on "World Vision," but he had no vision for the world because he learned these things in a quiet, academic atmosphere. Such a learning experience required no compassion for the lost, no sacrifice of life, no walk of faith—in fact, not much of anything except the discipline of one hour a week.

When it was all over, I saw that I had not extended the ministry and had done nothing to help solve the labor shortage. My problem was that I did not understand the place of evangelism in training laborers. I have since discovered that where there is no evangelism, there is a flat, tasteless, fizzless, mechanical ministry.

There are a few simple, positive steps the equipper can take as he seeks to combine an evangelistic outreach with training. These are proven methods for producing reproducers.

(1) The first key method is *field training*. Most churches have a visitors register. The resourceful equipper can use this to good advantage. Rather than calling on a visitor alone, he can take a budding laborer with him. On the first call or two the prospective laborer need do nothing but sit there and observe. After a few calls, the equipper can call on him to give a word of testimony. "Joe, you became a Christian a few months ago. Why don't you share with us just how that came about?" After the call

has been made, the equipper can discuss the young laborer's testimony, helping him improve it so that it communicates more clearly and effectively. It helps if he writes it out first. Then the equipper can make suggestions.

The next step is for the developing laborer to take the lead by actually sharing the gospel while the equipper looks on. Later, of course, the equipper can evaluate his presentation, making whatever suggestions are appropriate and necessary. Eventually, when the time is ripe, the laborer can begin to take someone with him to train in the ministry.

What comes out of all this? Compassion for the lost? Yes, I'm sure of it. God certainly wants his harvest laborers to have consistent exposure to needy people who are without hope because they are without Him. The Lord desires our hearts to be moved with compassion. What about the value of Scripture memory? Yes, most definitely. The laborer becomes aware of just how valuable the memorized Word is when he is witnessing to a person who has questions about spiritual things. How about faith? Dependence on God? Prayer? Yes, these vital aspects of our walk with God are seen as absolute essentials.

When we learn our lessons out on the battlefield of the everyday world, we gain a new appreciation for what we have learned. Thus we come to see laboring in a different light than we see it in a basement while passing notebooks back and forth. Laboring should be a living reality, not an assortment of interesting spiritual information. That's why field training is such a vital part of developing laborers. Involvement in the equipper's life and ministry is the key to helping someone who is being trained to grasp the spiritual principles he is being taught.

(2) Another key in developing laborers is *prayer.* During our time in the Midwest with The Navigators, Virginia and I had a number of prospective laborers living in our home with us. These were young men I had met at schools throughout that

area who had shown a keen desire to become lifetime laborers in the kingdom of God. Today they are scattered around the world, giving their lives to other young people who evidence the desire to make an impact for Christ in a disciplemaking ministry.

Shortly after these men moved into our home, I memorized Exodus 17:11: "And it came to pass, when Moses held up his hand, that Israel prevailed: and when he let down his hand, Amalek prevailed." Joshua was locked in battle with Amalek, but Amalek was overcome by the power of prayer. I drew a spiritual application from the verse and began a practice that I believe God used to help these young men thrive and grow. Each morning I rose early and went to prayer. In my mind's eye I visualized each of these guys still asleep in bed. One by one I lifted them up before the throne of grace. Morning by morning I prayed for Bob, Jim, Larry, Don, Marvin, Russ, Carl, and Ray. While they slept, I visually picked them up from their beds, holding them up before the Lord in prayer. I have hesitated to share this because I know it sounds a bit odd. But I believe that those early morning prayers were used of God to help these men become devoted laborers in the overripe fields of the world.

(3) A third key to equipping is *serving as an example.* Jesus said to His disciples, "Follow me, and I will make you fishers of men" (Matthew 4:19). The equipper himself must model the message and the ministry of Jesus.

Jesus did not just say, "Listen to me." Many did that with great blessing and profit. But He went beyond words. He *lived* it.

Jesus furnished the example. He set the pace. This is tremendously significant when we remember what people said about His words: "No man ever spake like this man!" His words were "with power." Even so, Jesus did not say, "Listen to me." He said, "Follow me." Anyone who equips laborers should likewise serve as an example. The apostle Paul spelled out this principle in language that cannot be misunderstood: "Those things, which ye have both learned, and received, and heard, and seen in me, do: and the God of peace shall be with you" (Philippians 4:9).

Ultimately it is God Himself who develops laborers. Jesus said, "Ye have not chosen me, but I have chosen you, and ordained you, that ye should go and bring forth fruit, and that your fruit should remain: that whatsoever ye shall ask of the Father in my name, he may give it you" (John 15:16). God's supremacy in laboring manifests itself in many ways.

First, God chooses His people and sends them forth.

Second, He enables them to become "able ministers of the New Testament." "Not that we are sufficient of ourselves to think any thing as of ourselves; but our sufficiency is of God; who also hath made us able ministers of the new testament; not of the letter, but of the spirit: for the letter killeth, but the spirit giveth life" (2 Corinthians 3:5-6).

Third, it is the Lord who empowers laborers for the work He has for them. "We have this treasure in earthen vessels, that the excellency of the power may be of God, and not of us" (2 Corinthians 4:7).

Fourth, it is the Lord who helps laborers discover, use, and develop spiritual gifts. "Now there are diversities of gifts, but the same Spirit. And there are differences of administrations, but the same Lord. And there are diversities of operations, but it is the same God which worketh all in all. But the manifestation of the Spirit is given to every man to profit withal" (1 Corinthians 12:4-7).

The ministry of an equipper is a work of faith, a labor of love. His eyes are on the Lord and his heart goes out to those he is helping. As Paul told the Galatians, "By love serve one another" (Galatians 5:13). The equipper sees himself as a servant who is willing, for the sake of those he is helping, to "spend and be spent" (2 Corinthians 12:15). A self-centered person who is greedy for personal glory or gain cannot be an equipper. The kind of humility, sacrifice, and servant spirit modeled by Jesus are key ingredients to an effective equipping ministry, ingredients that are essential in producing dynamic spiritual workers who reproduce a perpetual harvest of laborers for the Lord.

CHAPTER ELEVEN

LIGHTING THE FIRE

God is in the business of giving life where there is no life. He uses certain people to rally others who lack incentive. The equipper—the one who trains laborers—must be a motivator. After all, laboring is hard work. Often when a laborer in training grows weary or discouraged, he is inclined to throw up his hands and leave the field. Yet if laborers are given the right kind of motivation from equippers, they can plow through the most awesome obstacles and keep going despite the most desperate circumstances.

During the Second World War, the Australian Navy recruited and trained a band of radio-equipped coastwatchers. With their binoculars, they manned their lookout points, reporting the Japanese naval, air, and troop movements. Everyone agreed that the reason for the remarkable success of this operation was the extraordinary bravery and motivation of these coast-watchers—local inhabitants of dozens of islands stretching across a 2,500 mile crescent of ocean from New Guinea to the New Hebrides.

Jacob Vonza was a scout who typified the kind of motivation and bravery for which these coastwatchers were famous. He was captured by a Japanese patrol upon returning from a mission on Guadalcanal in August of 1942. While the Japanese were strip-searching him, they discovered an American flag given to him by a United States Marine. The Japanese interrogated him, but he refused to answer their questions. They tied him to a tree and pounded him with the butts of their rifles. When he still refused to cooperate, his captors bayoneted him in the chest five times, slit his throat with a sword, and left him for dead. After the Japanese were out of sight, Jacob gnawed through the cords with which he had been tied to the tree. He half-staggered and half-crawled three miles to a Marine outpost. There, before collapsing from loss of blood, he gave the best report yet received of enemy strength on the island.

The Australian Navy will tell you that these coastwatchers saved Guadalcanal, and that the Guadalcanal operation saved the Pacific and stopped the Japanese thrust to Australia itself. The key to their brilliant and devoted service was their dedication, bravery, and motivation. When people are motivated, they can solve the most difficult problems and overcome the most trying obstacles.

I can give personal testimony to this fact. On September 15, 1943 I joined the Marines. During my days in boot camp in San Diego, I became aware of a much maligned group of people called "nonswimmers." These were the Marines in boot camp who failed the swimming test and were subsequently sent to a nonswimmer platoon, thus making it impossible for them to graduate from boot camp with their regular outfit. This demoting procedure was described by the drill instructor as a fate worse than death. There was not much in this world lower than a nonswimmer.

As I listened to the drill instructor, I knew that I had a problem: I couldn't swim. In fact, I had never been in water that was over my head. The only swimming I did in Neola, Iowa when I was growing up was in the ponds of stagnant water outside the town. I would splash around in these ponds with the rest of the kids and get pink eye, but I never learned how to swim.

Because I really wanted to graduate with my platoon, I determined I would try to pass the swimming test, which consisted of swimming to the far end of the pool and back. On the day of the test, we marched to the pool, and soon it came my turn to jump in. I did, fighting off fear and panic. I began to flail my arms and kick my legs, and to my surprise I made it to the far end.

As I turned to start back, I began to grow weary. I was tempted to give up. But I was creating such a splash in the water with my ungainly kicking and thrashing that the sergeant in charge became interested. He began to encourage me. He shouted into his megaphone, "Come on, boot, you can do it! Don't give up! Keep it up! Go! Go! Go!" Others joined him at the sides of the pool. Soon the whole platoon was cheering me on. I desperately wanted to make it. I knew that if I didn't, I wouldn't graduate with the guys I had come to know. I would be put back with a group of strangers where the only common experience was that they too were nonswimmers.

I pounded and kicked the water. I struggled and struggled, and I finally made it, amid the cheers of the sergeant with the megaphone and the men in my platoon. What a victory! The key to it all? I was motivated by a strong desire to stick with the guys in my own platoon and to never be known by the the U.S. Marine Corps as a nonswimmer. Motivation can determine the difference between winning and losing, victory and defeat. And sometimes it determines the difference between life and death.

The ancient Mayan Indians played a game in which a goal was scored by causing a ball to go through a ring high on a wall. But carvings depict something quite unique about the game: The captain of the losing team—or quite possibly the whole team—was sacrificed to the gods. One can only imagine the keen motivation present in those team members when they took to the field.

But what are the unique keys to motivating laborers? First of all, the equipper must himself embody the ideals of the person or group he is equipping for service. Paul reminded the Philippians that he had not only *taught* certain things but also *demonstrated* them in his own life (Philippians 4:9). The equipper must remember when he is working with a laborer that he needs to use a basic training program. But at the same time he must constantly keep in mind that he is not working with a robot. He is involved in the life of a human being. Therefore, his contact with the budding laborer cannot be merely on the technical level.

The equipper should plan some social events—having the laborer and his family over for an evening, going on hikes, attending sporting events, just plain having fun. The budding laborer will respond much more enthusiastically if he is treated as a human being rather than just a means of accomplishing the ministry.

Each laborer needs to catch Jesus' vision of the harvest. The equipper must help him realize that he is involved at a highly strategic level in the Great Commission of Jesus Christ. The focus of Christ's command is to make disciples. The key to accomplishing that mission is laborers. The laborer is thus the vital link in Christ's world mission. He is the one who invests his life in winning people to Christ and helping those who truly repent and believe to become mature, dedicated, fruitful disciples.

I know nothing more motivating than to realize that you are striking at the very heart of the Great Commission. The potential laborer must see his ministry as the essential operation that Jesus prayed for when He "saw the multitudes and was moved with compassion."

Even when someone becomes a spiritually qualified

laborer, the work is not finished. He needs periodic stimulation and encouragement. I recall a fellow I met with on a personal level for about two years who became a highly skilled laborer. His job took him away from fellowship with anyone of like heart. After some time the heavy load of his job, the demands of his supervisors, and the pressures of his peers bore down so heavily on him that he buckled under. His circumstances bent, shaped, and molded his Christian life so powerfully that to look at him and listen to him, one would be hard pressed to detect that he had once been involved in laboring.

The Bible says, "Let us hold fast the profession of our faith without wavering; (for he is faithful that promised;) and let us consider one another to provoke unto love and to good works" (Hebrews 10:23-24). In order to hold fast in this ministry, we need periodic stimulation to excite us to good works and hard labor. Sometimes we need someone to light a fire in our weary souls.

The time to teach the essentials of laboring is when the disciple is motivated and eager to learn. It is interesting to note Jesus' timing in teaching His disciples the Lord's Prayer. He had already preached sermons to them, taught them parables, and healed many people. He had stilled the tempest, cast out many demons, raised Jairus' daughter to life, and fed five thousand people. Then, finally, He taught them to pray (Luke 11:1-4).

Why did He wait so long to bring this vital imperative of discipleship to them? The answer is obvious. He waited until they asked, "Lord, teach us to pray." It does little good to go over all the various aspects of prayer with a person until the person is motivated to pray. To transfer notes about prayer from your notebook to someone else's does little more than increase his volume of spiritual knowledge. The time to teach is when the person will pick it up and put it to work. The equipper must be a motivator, stimulating a hunger in the laborer when he has no appetite.

Question: What should be the self-identity of the equipper? Answer: He should see himself as a servant. He must, like Paul, be willing to "spend and be spent" (2 Corinthians 12:15). He does not henceforth live unto himself (2 Corinthians 5:15, Romans 14:7-8). Rather, he sees his life as an investment. His overriding desire is to pass the life that Christ has given him into the lives of other men and women. His life is precious only as it is used by the blessed Holy Spirit to enrich others.

This kind of commitment is no easy task. Being a servant to others is costly. The equipper will be misunderstood, taken advantage of, and used. But he has a secret source of energy from which to draw the strength, patience, encouragement, and wisdom he needs. That source of strength is Christ's attitude of servanthood as revealed in Mark 10:45: "For even the Son of man came not to be ministered unto, but to minister, and to give his life a ransom for many."

More than just being a servant, the equipper is a teacher of servanthood. It is interesting to see how Jesus went about teaching what being a servant requires. He did something that His disciples would never be able to forget, something that you and I would never have thought of doing. He washed their feet. What a way to teach!

Let's say that you are blessed with a visit from a well-known Christian leader. On the way to the airport you drive through a rainstorm. You meet this person at the plane and load up the bags to drive to your home. After a chat in the living room, you are called to the kitchen to lend your wife a hand for a few minutes.

Upon returning to the living room, you discover that your guest has disappeared. You look outside, and to your amazement you see him out there washing your car, which had been speckled with mud on your trip to the airport. Would you ever forget that? No, and you would probably tell many other people of the humble, servant spirit you saw in action that day. Jesus was likewise a servant and a trainer of servants. The one who equips laborers thus has a powerful example to follow.

One day a fellow went to Dawson Trotman with a tale of woe. The person in whom he had been investing his life and for whom he had such high hopes had bailed out. The guy was crushed. "Oh, Daws," he asked, "what shall I do?" Daw's reply was succinct and to the point. "Get another!"

Exactly! In every battle there will be casualties. The wise equipper realizes that because he is in a spiritual battle, he can expect some casualties. Ours is not a game where polite gentlemen and ladies follow agreed-upon rules. Ours is a conflict with "the prince of darkness grim." Satan knows no rules, no mercy, no scruples. His nature is evil and his attacks are meant to cripple, maim, or kill. The equipper must be a kind of spiritual medic who does what he can to restore the wounded to fighting form, all the while on the alert for others who can fill the ranks.

Discouragement is the perpetual enemy of equippers. At times the ministry seems to resemble the recent tragedy on the Nile. Egyptians and Sudanese were on a boat on the Nile returning with a load of kerosene. When the ship caught fire, many leaped from the blazing ship into crocodile infested waters. Those who made it past the jaws of the crocodiles to the shore were attacked by poisonous scorpions that lined the bank.

When things used to go wrong in our family, my mother would say, "LeRoy, if it's not one thing it's two." That is often the way the ministry of the equipper appears. There are times when the equipper says to himself, "What else could possibly go wrong?"

It's rather like the Wycliffe missionary I read about recently. She was called late one night to help deliver a baby. One of the local women in the tribe was giving birth to her firstborn.

As the missionary was assisting in the early stages of the birth, a deadly poisonous snake dropped from the thatched roof of the hut to her left arm. The rule is that you remain perfectly still when such a snake is on you. But she couldn't; she had a baby to deliver. She shook loose from the snake, and the women who had gathered chased the snake away with sticks.

Shortly thereafter, the baby was delivered, but the missionary discovered it wasn't breathing. As she began mouth-to-mouth resuscitation, she discovered there was something clogging the throat of the baby. Just as she cleared the baby's throat, there was a scream from one of the women. Her hair was on fire because she had gotten too close to a candle. As some of the women doused the flames, the baby began to breathe. There, at last, was a healthy, beautiful baby in its mother's arms.

As I read this story, I said to myself, "That's exactly what it's like trying to bring a spiritually qualified laborer into the world." It seems like everything imaginable goes wrong. But the equipper must be a dogged soul. He must not be easily deterred, for the stakes are too high. Christ's kingdom must march forward. Yes, the battle will heat up. Yes, the devil will throw up every roadblock at his command. But the equipper must be *persistent.*

One more quality is necessary for the one who equips laborers: *transparency.* Paul repudiated a "cloak of covetousness." There was nothing the apostle was hiding. What was within him was lived out for all to see.

But the tendency ever since Adam and Eve has been for fallen man to hide from God. Jesus said, "This is the condemnation, that light is come into the world, and men loved darkness rather than light, because their deeds were evil. For every one that doeth evil hateth the light, neither cometh to the light, lest his deeds should be reproved" (John 3:19-20).

The life of the equipper is open and aboveboard. Like Paul

he has "renounced the hidden things of dishonesty, not walking in craftiness, nor handling the word of God deceitfully; but by manifestation of the truth commending [himself] to every man's conscience in the sight of God" (2 Corinthians 4:2). The people who are being trained can spot a fake. The equipper must never be afraid to share both his victories and defeats, his strengths and weaknesses. The budding laborer can learn from both. The equipper is a motivator and a servant who is persistent and transparent in his ministry for the Lord.

CHAPTER TWELVE

LIVING THE REALITY

A lifetime laborer in the kingdom of God is priceless. His potential for good is immeasurable. To try to calculate the impact of just one laborer whose life is lived for the gospel of Christ would drive a computer crazy. There are six points an equipper must keep in mind as he carefully prepares the disciple to become a dedicated lifetime laborer.

First of all, *The laborer must face up to the reality of what spiritual labor is all about.* When Paul told the Thessalonians, "Know them which labour among you" (1 Thessalonians 5:12), he used the word that signifies laboring to the point of exhaustion. God is looking for hard workers. There is no room for a lazy person in the ranks of His laborers. Thus the potential laborer must enter the field thoroughly prepared for what he will face. Laboring is for those who are not afraid of hard work, those who know exactly what they are getting into.

Last summer I had the joy of taking my family, including two granddaughters, to Disneyland. It was a fun day. We were met at the gate by Mickey Mouse, Goofey, Donald Duck, and others of the Disney family. It gave me a good feeling. Wholesome fun for the whole family.

As the day sped on I watched Mickey going up to children,

having his picture taken with them and doing all he could to bring a smile to their faces. I began to get a warm glow—a feeling of real appreciation for him. Mickey was a good guy.

After supper we were prepared to leave. The grandkids asked if they could take just a few more minutes to go up to the Swiss Family Robinson tree house. Of course. But I decided to wait for them at the bottom. So up they went, accompanied by Rich, their dad. As they had their fun, I rested at the bottom of the tree.

Suddenly from out of nowhere a mouse came scurrying across my path and leaped up my left trouser leg. I was terrified. I immediately jumped to my feet and began to shake my left leg. After what seemed an eternity, the mouse scurried back to the ground and disappeared into the bushes. My heart was pounding. People who were coming down the stairs from the tree house were amused and bewildered by my one-legged dance.

In a flash I saw that my affection for Mickey did not carry over to real mice. I don't want mice running up my leg. I don't like mice when they do that. There was a big difference between my attitude toward Mickey and my attitude toward that little gray critter that leaped on me. One I liked; the other I didn't.

The equipper needs to make sure that the prospective laborer does not live in a dream world—a laborer's fantasyland. The laborer must understand what it's really all about. The equipper must not paint a distorted picture in order to recruit more laborers. Those who enter the labor force under false pretenses or with false notions of what it's all about won't last. They need to enter the harvest field not with their head in the clouds but with their feet on the ground. *Reality* is the name of the game.

Once while in the river museum in Memphis, as I looked at the many pictures of the old Mississippi steamboats and admired the grand architecture, I was carried away with a mental picture of a beautiful, romantic time when these giant riverboats plied the waters. But a plaque along the wall jarred me back to reality. The plaque described how the boats would often capsize and sink. The steam boilers would often blow up, killing hundreds of people. The steamboat was generally considered to be a filthy form of transportation.

There was a vast difference between the myth and the fact. The equipper must dispel the myths and clearly state the facts about the ministry of laboring. He must know the reality.

The second point is closely related to the first: *The laborer must see beyond the hard work to the real beauty of the ministry of disciplemaking.* The laborer must never lose sight of the attractiveness of a life lived out in devoted discipleship to Christ. Yes, the work is filled with difficulties, but it's worth it. The most beautiful and precious thing in the sight of God is a life that honors His Son, a life that is lived to His glory.

The Karakum is in the heart of the Turkestan Desert. To see it is to hate it. Barren. Desolate. Foreboding. An English visitor said of the Karakum, "All other deserts are insignificant compared to this endless ocean of sand. I cannot imagine a sight more terrible." His reaction was typical. That's the way the Karakum strikes visitors. The thought of entering that empty wasteland strikes terror in the heart. There is nothing appealing about the place. Beauty is the last word that would come to mind.

Yet the nomads who roam there—the Tekins, the Salars, the Ersors, the Zomuds, the Karandashlis—would not live anywhere else than in their beloved Karakum. An old Karakum shepherd who had come out of the desert to visit the Ashkhabad bazaar said, "My heart bleeds for these poor people here who have never seen that beauty. Tomorrow, if Allah lets me sell my sheep, I will leave this den of iniquity and confusion and return to the desert splendor, where I shall pray to be permitted to die without ever seeing this sinful ugliness again."

Perhaps there is a remote picture here of the life of a laborer and the ministry of laboring. Most look at it and see only the heartache, the hard work, the long hours, and the difficulties involved. They would rather spend their days in a more conventional program. Fair enough—to each his own. But as I look back on the years spent as a common laborer and eventually as an equipper of others, I can think of no other ministry more beautiful. The changed lives, the delivered souls, the men and women who today are laboring around the world are all constant reminders of the grace and goodness of God.

Each equipper must help the prospective laborer face the reality of the work. But let him also help the person see beyond all of the drudgery to the joys that await his investment of life. Even more important than seeing the reality is *living* the reality. As the apostle John said, "I have no greater joy than to hear that my children walk in truth" (3 John 4). The apostle Paul put it like this: "What is our hope, or joy, or crown of rejoicing? Are not even ye in the presence of our Lord Jesus Christ at his coming? For ye are our glory and joy" (1 Thessalonians 2:19-20).

Third, *The prospective laborer must fully weigh the options.* What else is out there? What other ministries could he enter? For those who have soul-winning and follow-up on their hearts, the answer is clear: Become a laborer. For those who have other pursuits at the top of their priority list, let them pursue those matters. But for the person who wants to give his life to winning the lost and edifying the saved, helping them become mature, dedicated, motivated disciples, there is one obvious course to follow: Become a spiritually qualified laborer. It is the responsibility of the equipper to make sure that his understudy has this full-orbed perspective.

Fourth, *God continually tests the faith of the laborer.* Laboring is what Paul described as a "work of faith" (1 Thessalonians 1:3). The laborer, who is a fisher of men, should remember that fishing is an act of faith. There are no guarantees for the fisherman. Sometimes there is a catch and sometimes there isn't.

The life of a farmer is also a life of faith. Sometimes the field produces a crop and sometimes it doesn't. Sometimes there are abundant harvests and sometimes there are crop failures. In spiritual laboring there are both victories and trials. The Lord continually gives us tests of faith to help us become stronger and more useful for Him.

Some time ago I was teaching on the life of Elijah in one of the adult Sunday school classes in our church. As I prepared for the class, I wondered about the tests of faith that believers encounter. Does there ever come a time in our walk with the Lord that those trials end? Does there come a time for the laborer when his faith will no longer be tested? I don't think so. An incident in the life of Elijah clearly points this out.

Let's say that a friend of yours invites you to his home for lunch. He suggests that you go in his car, but when you get to the parking lot you discover that his car is on fire. He seems not to notice and says to you, "Okay, hop in and we'll go out to my place for lunch."

What would your reaction be? Probably you would stop and say, "I'm not getting in there." "Why not?" he asks. "Well," you say, "as you can see, it's burning up!"

But this was the very thing that God told Elijah to do! Note 2 Kings 2:11: "And it came to pass, as they still went on, and talked, that, behold, there appeared a chariot of fire, and horses of fire, and parted them both asunder; and Elijah went up by a whirlwind into heaven." Incredible!

Remember, these prophets, Elijah and Elisha, were men "subject to like passions as we are" (James 5:17). Do you think

Elijah may have hesitated for a moment before jumping into the midst of that chariot of fire? The last act in the life of Elijah was a test of faith. Would he trust God to keep him even in the midst of the fire? You and I have a clear picture here of our walk with God. If a person says "I love God" or "I trust Him," God will give that person an opportunity to prove it—right down to the end. Let the laborer rest assured that there will be both successes and failures in his fishing for men, and enough work in the fields for all the days of his life.

Fifth, *A laborer needs to see the imperative of holiness.* God cannot use a filthy life to make disciples. To prepare himself for the work of laboring, the disciple must purge himself "from all filthiness of the flesh and spirit, perfecting holiness in the fear of God" (2 Corinthians 7:1). Only then will he be "a vessel unto honour, sanctified, and meet for the master's use, and prepared unto every good work" (2 Timothy 2:21).

This truth was brought forcefully to my attention some years ago. I was on a preaching mission in a less developed area of the world. One day I was traveling along a road that followed a river. The people who lived beside the river were using it for various functions: as drinking water, as bathing water, as a toilet, and as water for washing clothes. As I watched the women do their laundry in that river, I became aware of the fact that they were not going to get those clothes clean no matter how hard they pounded or rubbed. Clothes do not come clean in filthy water.

I was speaking to a group of laborers that day and reminded them of that fact. God is looking in His labor force for people who are holy. "If we confess our sins, he is faithful and just to forgive us our sins, and to cleanse us from all unrighteousness" (1 John 1:9). "Come out from among them, and be ye separate, saith the Lord, and touch not the unclean thing; and I will receive you, and will be a Father unto you, and ye shall be my sons and daughters, saith the Lord Almighty" (2 Corinthians 6:17-18). A holy life is a powerful weapon in the hand of a holy God.

"And when he had called the people unto him with his disciples also, he said unto them, Whosoever will come after me, let him deny himself, and take up his cross, and follow me" (Mark 8:34). This is perhaps the most difficult concept of all for the laborer: *A laborer is one who has determined to give his life to others.* Obviously, therefore, *he cannot live for self.*

But rejecting the interests of self is hard. And self does not take it lying down. Self will argue, cajole, and plead. Self will remind us, "But we've known each other for so long! We've had such good times together. Remember the good old days." But the words of Jesus are clear. *Deny self.* This is a critical step for the disciple who has committed himself to becoming a laborer living for others.

You and I may never die a martyr's death or wear a martyr's crown, but we can plead with God for a martyr's heart. Oh, the honor, the inestimable honor of being permitted to carry on a work so near to the heart of God! It is amazing that the Lord would entrust such a precious mission to the likes of us. And when we look back through the wonders of eternity, we can only wish that we had done more, sacrificed more, prayed more, labored more. These are the factors that will shine like diamonds on the pages of our lives. And the "well done" of Jesus will make that life commitment worth it all.